T0345081

Experimenting with Religion

Experimenting with Religion

The New Science of Belief

JONATHAN JONG

OXFORD
UNIVERSITY PRESS

OXFORD
UNIVERSITY PRESS

Oxford University Press is a department of the University of Oxford. It furthers
the University's objective of excellence in research, scholarship, and education
by publishing worldwide. Oxford is a registered trade mark of Oxford University
Press in the UK and certain other countries.

Published in the United States of America by Oxford University Press
198 Madison Avenue, New York, NY 10016, United States of America.

© Oxford University Press 2023

All rights reserved. No part of this publication may be reproduced, stored in
a retrieval system, or transmitted, in any form or by any means, without the
prior permission in writing of Oxford University Press, or as expressly permitted
by law, by license, or under terms agreed with the appropriate reproduction
rights organization. Inquiries concerning reproduction outside the scope of the
above should be sent to the Rights Department, Oxford University Press, at the
address above.

You must not circulate this work in any other form
and you must impose this same condition on any acquirer.

Library of Congress Cataloging-in-Publication Data
Names: Jong, Jonathan, author.
Title: Experimenting with religion : the new science of belief / Jonathan Jong.
Description: New York, NY : Oxford University Press, [2023] |
Includes bibliographical references and index.
Identifiers: LCCN 2022054439 (print) | LCCN 2022054440 (ebook) |
ISBN 9780190875541 (hb) | ISBN 9780190875565 (epub) | ISBN 9780197677568
Subjects: LCSH: Religiousness. | Psychometrics.
Classification: LCC BV4509.5 .J665 2023 (print) | LCC BV4509.5 (ebook) |
DDC 200.1/9—dc23/eng/20230110
LC record available at https://lccn.loc.gov/2022054439
LC ebook record available at https://lccn.loc.gov/2022054440

DOI: 10.1093/oso/9780190875541.001.0001

Printed by Sheridan Books, Inc., United States of America

For Ella Mae, my one; and Edith, ours

Contents

Preface and acknowledgments

This is not a book about religion. There is a lot about religion in it, but it is really a book about science. More specifically, it is a book about experimental psychology, and how a group of experimental psychologists have used the tools of this trade to study religion as a human phenomenon. For the past decade, I have counted myself lucky to join these scientists in the pursuit of understanding how and why people believe in things like gods, souls, and rituals. I am additionally grateful for their time and cooperation as I was writing this book, without which it would not have been possible. In an important way, this book is as much about them as about their research. Special thanks, then, to Will Gervais, Bob Calin-Jageman, Deborah Kelemen, Justin Barrett, Bruce Hood, Nathalia Gjersoe, Ben Purzycki, Cristine Legare, Ken Vail III, and Brittany Cardwell for speaking with me at length. I hope not to have misrepresented them in any way in retelling their stories.

As far as I can tell from my limited powers of introspection, there are two motivations behind this book. The first is my desire to assess this field of research—the psychology of religion—especially in light of recent developments in psychology more broadly. As I cover in greater detail in the opening chapters of this book (and especially in Chapter 2), psychology is currently undergoing a crisis of confidence, and perhaps rightly so. I wanted to take a close and sober look at the work we have done so far to figure out whether we have just been wasting our time, applying egregiously inadequate methods to our research questions. And even if we haven't, I wanted to think through the challenges we will need to meet to do a better job than we have done. Admittedly, this seems like inside baseball. The second reason for writing this book is less insular.

The emphasis when presenting scientific research to the general public is almost always, understandably on the *discoveries* themselves. But this leaves out the *process* of scientific discovery, from the conception of the hypothesis to the design of the experiment, the analysis of the data, and the eventual publication of the paper. This is what I want to focus on: I want to give people a sense of what it is like to do science, to be a scientist behind the discoveries. Frankly, I don't know if any of the findings presented in this book will stand the test of time, and it is not my intention to present any of them as solid and undisputed fact. Rather, what I hope you take away from the book is an appreciation for science as a human endeavor—a social endeavor, even—to understand the world and ourselves.

Such an appreciation for the human and social side of science is, I believe, important for cultivating a healthy *trust* in science. As I am writing this preface, the world is still slowly emerging from the COVID-19 pandemic, and it has been interesting—if also vexing—to observe the various interactions between science and society. There has been alarming skepticism over vaccines, for example; and also a lot of anger over mask mandates and lockdowns. Some of this anger has been a reaction against *changes* in policy, which were sometimes (though not always) informed by changes in the scientific consensus. Frustrations were, more often than not, directed toward politicians, but scientists were also accused of ignorance and fickleness.

But, from the perspective of a scientist, the changes in scientific consensus (and subsequent changes in policy and advice) were totally predictable. When the pandemic first began, before there was much good data about COVID-19 specifically, scientists gave advice based on what they knew about previous pandemics; as they discovered more and more about COVID-19, they could update the advice they were giving. And learning more about COVID-19 also involved learning more about how to learn about COVID-19: what the best questions to ask were, and how best to answer them.

I feel even more strongly now than I did when I first began writing this book that a better understanding of *how* scientists work is crucial for setting appropriate expectations about scientific discoveries, which are always provisional and partial. It is something of a joke among scientists that the conclusion to every research project is always "more research is required." But like all good jokes, this one is predicated on something true.

I owe my interest in the processes of science to a philosopher rather than to any scientist: Alan Musgrave, who taught me history and philosophy of science at the University of Otago. I cannot say that we agree, either about science or about religion, but his lectures have remained with me, and have found their way into this book. When I needed help with the physics, my friend Timothy Prisk stepped in to give me crash courses on demand. Neither of them is to blame for any errors I have made.

My fascination with religion has deeper and more personal roots, and there is a moderately worrying sense in which my academic research has been an exercise in narcissistic navel-gazing. Once upon a few years ago, I thought

I had to choose between an academic career in psychology and a life of service as a priest: the Bishop of Dunedin at the time, the Right Reverend Dr Kelvin Wright, would have none of this and sent me packing to Oxford to take up a postdoctoral position. He arranged for me to be trained in Oxford alongside my job, and I was ordained at the Cathedral here a few years later. Ever since, I have managed to live a rich life in two parts. I do not know if my scientific research contributes in any way to my work as a priest, but I can say with some confidence that parish work reminds me daily why I am a psychologist of religion. It is easy for psychologists to fall into the habit of thinking of people as cells in a spreadsheet or points on a graph, as "participants" or worse still "subjects." But my parishioners are very obviously people, with earnest faiths and real doubts: and if the psychology of religion is not fundamentally about them and people like them around the world, then it's not at all obvious what it is about or indeed what it is for.

Several institutions have supported me as I wrote this book. The Centre for Trust, Peace and Social Relations at Coventry University adopted me as my previous department was shut down under slightly dubious circumstances. The School of Anthropology and Museum Ethnography and St Benet's Hall at Oxford have also been welcoming homes-away-from-institutional-home. The John Templeton Foundation and the Templeton World Charity Foundation have both supported my work on this book in various ways, directly and indirectly. The former funded the *Think Write Publish: Science and Religion* project based at Arizona State University. The idea for this book grew into something real while I was a Fellow in this program, with thirteen other brilliant writers. I am grateful to Lee Gutkind and Daniel Sarewitz for electing me to the fellowship, and to Tobias Tanton, who suggested that I apply.

Joan Bossert at Oxford University Press very kindly invited me to submit a book proposal based on a very brief message, and Abby Gross and Nadina Persaud then helped me to develop it into something worth publishing. I am particularly indebted to the anonymous reviewers they appointed, whose suggestions I have incorporated as much and as best as I knew. This book has also been immeasurably improved by Tobias and Sarah Tanton, Adam Baimel, Peter Hill, Emily Burdett, and Emma Pritchard, who took the time to read drafts of it.

A lot has happened in my life in the five years since I first pitched this book to Oxford University Press (OUP), but none more important than my marriage to Ella Mae Lewis. We had our first date in Washington, DC, in

May 2017: she was in town for a conference about human trafficking, and I had just come into town for a conference on the cognitive science of belief at Georgetown. We then met up in London, Berlin, and Oxford before deciding that we had had enough of this peripatetic romance. We were married in January 2019 at St Mary Magdalen's parish church in Oxford. OUP was kind enough to allow me a deadline extension as a wedding present. Our daughter Edith was born a little over a year later. It is to them both that this book is dedicated.

Michaelmas Term
2022

1

(How) can psychologists study religion?

It did not take long for me to decide that social psychology was the science of everything that was interesting about people. Like all undergraduate psychology majors, I was taught the classics: Stanley Milgram's obedience studies, Leon Festinger's cognitive dissonance research, Jane Elliott's *Blue Eye-Brown Eyes* classroom activity on prejudice, Donald Dutton and Arthur Aron's *Suspension Bridge* experiment on romantic attraction, John Darley and Daniel Batson's *Good Samaritan* study on the bystander effect, and so on. I won't spoil them for you—information about them is easy enough to find[1]—except to say that they shone a piercing light for me into human nature. By my second year as an undergraduate, I was a born-again experimental social psychologist, utterly convinced that this was the best way to understand how people's minds work. Soon thereafter I began running my own experiments. Then, as now, my interests were broad. I ran studies on beauty and humor before landing on religion as a central focus. Religion, humor, beauty, morality, romance, prejudice, obedience: see what I mean about social psychology being the science of everything that is interesting about people?

A lot has changed since I was a student, not only within myself but also across my field. As we will explore further in the next chapter, there was a sort of crisis of confidence in social psychology just as I was leaving graduate school. This crisis and the revolution that it sparked made us question a lot of what we thought we knew, including from those classic studies that converted me to psychology in the first place. It even made us question *whether* psychologists are up to the job of shining light into human nature at all, and if so, *how*?

This book is an attempt to grapple with this question, if not necessarily to answer it. It is a sort of critical meditation on experimental psychology: our methods, their strengths and limitations, and the insight they can or cannot provide about why people do and say and think and feel the way they do. There are, broadly speaking, two ways to write a book like this. I could have sampled a broad array of topics in psychology—religion, humor, beauty, and

Experimenting with Religion. Jonathan Jong, Oxford University Press. © Oxford University Press 2023.
DOI: 10.1093/oso/9780190875541.003.0001

so forth—to consider the breadth of what psychological experimentation can tell us, perhaps even comparing them to experiments from other scientific fields: Galileo dropping balls of different weights off the Leaning Tower of Pisa to disprove Aristotle's theory of gravity, Antoine Lavoisier burning metals in bell jars to discover the role of oxygen in combustion, Thomas Young shining light through two vertical slits to show that light can behave like a wave, and the like. (I should note that Galileo probably never ran the experiment attributed to him, and Young may not have either.[2]) It would have been perfectly reasonable to write about the most important experiments in psychology but this has been done several times before.[3] Besides, it seemed to me both more interesting and more rigorous a test to home in on one phenomenon, and see how far experimental psychologists can go in helping us understand it.

Religion is the phenomenon that interests me most. I have spent my entire career trying to understand where it comes from. Most religious traditions have their own stories about this, of course. Roughly speaking, they all say that their own faiths began when the gods revealed themselves to specially chosen people, whereas other faiths are the product of human folly or the schemes of malevolent beings, or a combination of the two. Two observations may be made about these kinds of explanations. The first is that they are at least in part the purview of historians, who are better placed than I am to evaluate the historical veracity of stories about Moses and a burning bush, Siddartha Gautama meditating under a Bo tree, or Muhammad praying in a cave on Jabal al-Nour.

The second observation is that even if we believed these stories—even if we believed that YHWH spoke to Moses, Brahmā Sahampati to Siddartha, and the angel Jibrīl to Muhammad—we would still be left with questions about the human side of these interactions. What is it about the human mind that allowed these people to *believe* that they had spoken to gods and angels? And what is it about the human mind that has made billions and billions of people since believe these stories? This is where psychologists come in.

Francis Galton on prayer and longevity

There are many ways in which psychologists go about trying to figure out stuff, and this book is really only about one of them: *experiments*. There will therefore be no stories about psychoanalysts asking people reclined on couches about their relationships with their mothers. Nor will there be anything about monks meditating in neuroimaging machines. The first approach is a relic of the past, fortunately; the second is still very much in its infancy, especially when it comes to studies on religion. There is, however, a very common and useful method that will be largely sidelined here, that is the *correlational study*.

As far as I can tell, the first-ever application of statistics to the study of religion was Francis Galton's 1872 *Statistical Inquiries into the Efficacy of Prayer*, which is a sort of crude correlational study.[4] Galton was a genius, though seemingly quite a different sort of genius from his cousin Charles Darwin. Where Darwin was focused on his grand theory, Galton was a bit of a dabbler. Or, to put things in a more positive light, he was a polymath, who practically invented meteorology, forensic science, and behavioral genetics, among other things. He also made great contributions to statistics and was a pioneer of correlational research.

A correlation describes how closely two things are related to one another. For example, if we want to know whether tall people also tend to weigh more, we can collect data about people's heights and weights and calculate the correlation between them. Galton was the first to apply this technique to studying humans, not only our physical traits like height and weight, but also psychological ones like personality and intelligence. Unfortunately, he also used these techniques to promote eugenics, which he also invented, coining the term in 1833.

Galton wanted to know whether people who received more prayers also enjoyed longer lives. Galton did not have quantitative data about how often different individual people were the subjects of others' prayers, but it was common knowledge that prayers for certain social classes of people were obligatory. Prayers for the members of European royal families, for example, were standard elements of Christian worship. This is still true even now: a prayer "for the King's majesty" is still in the Church of England's Book of Common Prayer, though this is much less commonly used than it was in Galton's day. With this in mind, Galton managed to find lifespan data for several classes of people, including members of royal houses. Looking at these, he found that they lived no longer than other "eminent men," such as gentry and aristocracy, or indeed clergy, lawyers, doctors, military officers, traders, artists, and scholars. There was, in other words, no *positive correlation* between being prayed for and living longer. If anything, they enjoyed *shorter* lifespans, even when excluding deaths by accident or violence. Members of royal houses averaged about 64 years, compared to other classes of people who tended to make it beyond 67. From this, he concluded that prayer does not work, at least not to lengthen lives.

Admittedly, this was not the most sophisticated study. These days, it would probably have been rejected from scientific journals on straightforward methodological grounds. For starters, Galton's sample was not at all representative of the general population: it was composed entirely of famous people whose lives were recorded in biographical dictionaries. Galton essentially conducted Wikipedia research. Furthermore, and more seriously, Galton's study also suffers from what we call *confounding variables*. The problem is that members of royal houses probably differed from other people—even other eminent individuals—in a variety of ways besides the extents to which they were the subjects of people's prayers. Galton concluded that prayer simply does not work to prolong lives, but it is possible that kings and queens are, for genetic or lifestyle reasons, more likely than others to die young. Perhaps the prayers do work, but just not enough to compensate for the negative health effects of inbreeding and excess. Galton thought this possibility implausible but could not rule it out.

All correlational studies suffer from this latter limitation. Very good correlational studies try to account for confounding variables by measuring them and statistically "controlling" for them. More often than not, however, they provide less certainty than scientists would like for questions like Galton's about the effects and efficacies of things from prayers to pills. This is where experiments come in.

The Great Prayer Experiment

The experiment is the poster child of science. This is not because it is the only way to do science, but because it is a uniquely powerful method for looking at causes and effects. If Galton wanted more certainty about the efficacy of prayer or lack thereof, he should have run an experiment. The most recent and rigorous example of a scientific experiment—or *randomized control trial*, as they say in clinical contexts—on the efficacy of prayer was published in 2006 by a team led by Herbert Benson at the Harvard Medical School.[5] It is sometimes dubbed the "Great Prayer Experiment" because of its scale.

The experiment involved 1,802 coronary artery bypass surgery patients across six hospitals. Instead of trying to *measure* how much or how often they were prayed for, Benson's team decided to *manipulate* the dose of prayer each patient received. This—manipulation—is the essential difference between an experiment and a correlational study. Correlational studies observe the variation that exists in the world; experimental studies control conditions and examine what changes result. Conditions can be manipulated either *between-subjects* or *within-subjects*.[6] A study with a between-subjects design involves comparing different individuals or groups. When I was in school, the standard example involved two pots containing identical amounts of the same soil and water, into which were planted identical amounts of the same seed: one was exposed to sunlight while the other was kept in the dark, and—lo!—the former sprouted and grew, while the other remained dormant.

The classic example of a within-subjects experiment is a bit like an infomercial for exercise equipment, in that it involves before and after measurements, sandwiched between which is the experimental manipulation. Psychologists tend not to like this particular setup because we worry that participants don't respond well to being asked the same questions twice. The more common kind of within-subjects experiment in psychology is like shopping for a wedding cake: it involves exposing each participant to a whole bunch of different things that vary in just a handful of ways in different combinations. In the case of a wedding cake, this allows us to work out what traits—texture, sweetness, type of icing, and so forth—we like, even if our ideal cake was not among the ones we tried. Now that I think about it, maybe only experimentalists shop for wedding cakes this way.

The Great Prayer Experiment was a between-subjects study. Benson's team randomly allocated the patients into three groups: these three groups were then subjected to slightly different experimental conditions. This is the "random" part of a randomized control trial. Random allocation is a common way of making the groups as comparable as possible to begin with, so that the researchers can be sure that whatever changes emerge at the end of the study are due to the experimental conditions, and not to preexisting differences between groups. Random allocation makes it very unlikely that there are, for example, more genetically compromised and sedentary kings and queens in one of the groups than in the others. More importantly for this experiment, it makes it unlikely that patients in one group start off less healthy than those in the others. Benson's team actually checked for this and found that the three groups were indeed very well matched in terms of their cardiovascular history as well as their sex and age distributions.

Next, they told the first two groups of patients that they *might* receive prayers from others. Only one of these groups—the "experimental" or "treatment" group—actually did receive prayers; the other—the "control" group (hence, randomized *control* trial)—did not. The praying was done by three Christian organizations, which received a list of names of people for whom to pray that they might have "a successful surgery with a quick, healthy recovery and no complications." So, we have two groups of people, well matched in terms of age, sex, and cardiovascular health, all of whom knew they might be prayed for, but only one group of which in fact received additional prayers. I say "additional" prayers because Benson's team did not prohibit other people—family and friends, and so forth—from praying for the patients. Almost everyone expected that at least some family and friends would be praying for them, so this is really an experiment about the efficacy of extra prayers by strangers. Anyway, the point is that the only meaningful difference between these two groups of patients is that one of them received extra prayers. This then is the main experimental manipulation in this study. If Benson's group discovered that, at the end of the experiment, those patients were better off, then it is reasonable to conclude that the manipulation—the extra prayers—was what made the difference.

This is not what they discovered. They observed the patients for 30 days after the surgery and found no differences between the patients who received extra prayers and those who did not. The patients in the treatment group were not any less likely to die, nor were they less likely to suffer health complications within the 30-day period. You might say that the Great Prayer Experiment vindicated Galton's sketchy study. It also found something else, in the third group of patients. Unlike in the other two groups, these patients were told that they *would* be prayed for, and indeed were: Benson's team did not lie to them. This was their second experimental manipulation. Like the first group of patients, this third group received prayers: unlike the first group of patients, this third group were assured of extra prayers. This added assurance seems to have had an adverse effect: 8% of patients in this group suffered more health complications than the other two groups. So, prayers did not make things any better, but awareness of prayers seems to have made things worse!

We still don't know why Benson's third group suffered more complications than the other two groups. It could just have been a statistical fluke, a "chance finding" as Benson's team put it. For example, despite randomly allocating people into groups and checking that the groups were similar in various ways, it is still possible that the third group of patients started off more sus-ceptible to health complications than the others in some way that Benson's team had not considered. This sort of thing happens sometimes, even in very big studies. This is one reason for attempting to replicate experiments, and not to put too much stock in the findings of any single study.

It is also possible that knowing that they were the beneficiaries of extra prayers affected the patients in some way. It may have made them overconfi-dent and therefore more reckless about their diet as they were recuperating, for example. Or, quite the opposite, it may have made them more anxious, which may in turn have had adverse effects on their health. As one of the researchers in Benson's team mused at a press conference, "The patient might think, 'Am I so sick that they have to call in the prayer team?'"[7]

Some people balk at the idea that scientific studies—correlational, experi-mental, or otherwise—can show us whether or not prayers work. I probably should have started with a less controversial example than the Benson ex-periment, but I could not resist the temptation. I confess that I am somewhat sympathetic to this reaction, largely on theological grounds. According to most Christian theologians—and almost certainly also Jewish and Muslim ones, though I know much less about them—prayers only work when God wills them to. Furthermore, God can act for the good health of anyone even in the absence of prayers offered. If so, then we should not necessarily expect that prayer will necessarily confer health benefits. Without access to data about God's will, the tools of science are unable to answer the question. This line of reasoning is sound as far as it goes, but I do also worry that it goes too far. According to the same theologians—and indeed to mainstream Jewish, Christian, and Muslim teaching more generally—*nothing* happens except as willed by God. And yet, this should not stop us from being able to learn about causes and effects in the natural world via experiment. Gravity does not work unless God wills it to, but no one thinks that we need data about God's will to run experiments on general relativity. Perhaps prayer is a special case: or per-haps this is just a case of special pleading.

Psychologists are, broadly speaking, less interested in whether prayers work than in why people believe that they do. We are not interested in studying the will of the gods; rather, we are interested in people's beliefs about gods, including beliefs about what gods will. In this way, the psychology of religion is no different from the psychology of any other aspect of human life. Some psychologists study people's political beliefs; others study people's moral beliefs; we study people's religious beliefs. Now, some people are probably also going to balk at the idea that scientific studies can get at the causes of their religious beliefs: perhaps this too is a special case, like prayer. I'm afraid I don't have very much to say to such people, except to note that they rarely have any problem with scientists trying to investigate other people's religious beliefs.

Fortunately, this hardline view is not very widely held, even among religious folk. Most people are perfectly happy with the idea that some people might be more receptive to religious ideas than others, and that some religious ideas are more compelling than others, and that religious changes might happen more frequently in some stages of life than others, and that certain life events might lead people toward faith or away from it. Some religious people are even quite keen to find answers to these sorts of questions because they might prove useful to their respective religious causes. In fact, the earliest psychologists—in the late 19th century and early 20th century in the United States—shared this mindset as they researched things like religious conversion in adolescence and the role of religious experiences in moral development. This attitude cuts both ways, of course. Atheist activists might also be interested in finding out more about what causes religious belief, so that they can nip it in the bud. In any case, and mostly for reasons of intellectual curiosity rather than practical utility, these are exactly the sorts of ideas that psychologists are interested in exploring.

In the following chapters, we will encounter rather a lot of studies, but the main focus is on seven experiments. These are all experiments in the sense that the Great Prayer Experiment is an experiment. In each case, something is being manipulated and something else—usually a belief—is then measured. There is one crucial difference between the experiments covered in this book and Benson's Great Prayer Experiment, besides the shift in subject matter. It is, in some ways, the great challenge of psychological research more generally: measurement.

Psychological measurement

Galton and Benson had it easy: both wanted to measure when someone had died. It is true that there are multiple biomedical definitions of "death," and also multiple calendric systems with which to count one's age at death. Even so, once researchers decide on a definition, there are standardized and well-understood methods of determining when someone has died. We know how to observe whether someone's heart is beating unaided, or whether there is any spontaneous activity in their brainstem. We also know how to compute someone's age, whether it's on the Gregorian solar calendar or a Chinese lunar one. Even debates about when life begins do not really pose a problem for measurement, as long as we apply a single definition to all cases. Dating life from birth is obviously quite easy: but we are also very good at accurately estimating the date of conception now. Assessments of patients' health complications do require some thought about what counts as a complication: fortunately, the Society of Thoracic Surgeons has a standard definition, which Benson's team followed.

In principle, this is how psychological measurement works too. Measurement is the practical manifestation of definition. First, we need some working definition of the thing we want to measure. Here we face our first problem. The question "Why are people religious?" turns out to be too vague, because the term "religious" can mean several different things. Our religious identities, behaviors, and beliefs are not entirely unrelated to one another, but nor are they quite the same thing. Many people in Britain identify as Christian, for example, but have neither any firm theological beliefs nor any regular religious practices. Others regularly engage in practices like prayer and meditation without identifying with the religious traditions from which these practices emerged. Still others hold more-or-less inchoate supernatural beliefs—about a higher power or life after death or whatever—without either identifying with a religious tradition or engaging much with religious practices.

As we touched on briefly earlier, "religion" is hardly the only word that carries multiple meanings: "death" does too. But in the case of death, we can clearly delineate between cardiopulmonary and brain death and understand the relationship between them. The situation is quite different for the various aspects and types of religiosity. Most psychologists distinguish between religious beliefs, behaviors, identities, and experiences: but there is no consensus on what these things are, let alone how to measure them. What we do agree on is that, with the exception of behavior, they are not directly observable. We can hear a heart beating through a stethoscope, and therefore detect its cessation: not so for a belief or an emotional experience, religious or otherwise. We can directly hear what people say and watch what they do, but we all know that people's words and actions are not always accurate representations of their thoughts and feelings. All the same, behavior—including verbal behavior—is often the best access we have into people's

minds. Almost all psychological measurement is really measurement of behavior that we interpret as telling us something about what's going on in
people's heads.

So far it sounds as if "psychological measurement" is just a fancy way
of talking about what everyone does in our everyday social interactions.
We are constantly observing how people behave to guess at what they are
thinking, how they are feeling, and what they want. If psychologists are
better at mind-reading than other folks are, it can only be because we have
learned how to ask good questions and how to interpret answers. The skill of
asking questions well is one we share with other social scientists, of course,
as well as with journalists. Like journalists, some social scientists—chiefly
anthropologists—ask questions in the context of a face-to-face interview or something similar. Psychologists, like many sociologists, political
scientists, and behavioral economists, mostly ask people questions through
questionnaires, superficially similar to the quizzes that pop up all the time on
social media.

Among the many things psychologists study are the ways in which the
phrasing of questions, the format in which they are presented, and the context in which they are asked affect people's answers. We, and other social
scientists, benefit from this research: it helps us to ask better questions and
to watch out for sources of bias or error. The most famous of these errors is
probably the *leading question*. Consider the following question:

What is your religion?

This question simply assumes that the respondent has a religion. Even if
"none" is an option, the way the question is asked implies that the respondent
should mention something like Christianity or Buddhism. This in turn
means that it is likely to lead to overestimations of the number of religious
people in the sample. Unfortunately, this kind of question is quite common.
This exact question was used in the United Kingdom's most recent census
for England and Wales. A better way of asking the same question might be to
first ask

Do you regard yourself as belonging to any particular religion?

before asking those who respond "Yes" about their specific religious identities, which the British Cohort Study has commendably done. Comparisons

of the two methods show a substantial difference in the number of nonreligious individuals counted, so it is clear that the phrasing of the question does matter.[8]

There are other sources of error and bias besides leading questions, and the one that is perhaps most pertinent to psychologists of religion is *cultural* bias. Even psychological phenomena long considered to be universal turn out to vary across cultures. The Müller-Lyer optical illusion, for example—where two identical horizontal lines appear as if they are of different lengths—is greater in some cultures than in others.[9] Clinical diagnoses of psychological disorders also require cultural sensitivity, as different symptoms emerge in different contexts. Psychosis, for example, presents very differently in the United States than it does in India and Ghana.[10] Indeed, even within cultures there can be differences between groups, such as gender differences in symptoms for autism.[11] Intelligence testing—the use of IQ tests like the Weschler Adult Intelligence Scale (WAIS), especially in clinical and educational contexts—has also been subject to criticism for cultural bias, and the makers of such tests have made efforts to make more *culture free* tests.

If optical illusions, psychological disorders, and basic cognitive abilities are shaped by the cultures we inhabit, then things like religion are even more obviously so. Religious beliefs, rituals, and organizational structures obviously vary across cultures, and this diversity raises real challenges for measurement. Consider the seemingly simple question of how religious someone is. Not only are there multiple criteria for religiousness, but these differ from tradition to tradition. American evangelical Christians might emphasize private prayer and the reading of Scripture; Israeli Orthodox Jews might emphasize the observance of dietary rules; Malaysian Chinese folk religionists might emphasize the veneration of ancestors and the *feng shui* consultation. Even if we were to focus on a single religious behavior like prayer in Galton's study, we might need to be more specific about what we mean across religious traditions: some prayers are conversational and others formal, and these might not be comparable phenomena. The challenge of cross-cultural measurement used to be the special concern of cross-cultural psychologists, but as societies pluralize and cultures mingle, issues of cultural bias are becoming more relevant to us all.

What makes a good psychological measure?

I love online quizzes. I know which Hogwarts house I belong to, according to the Pottermore quiz (Slytherin: make of that what you will). I know which Disney Princess I am, according to Buzzfeed (Belle: make of *that* what you will). Then, there are quizzes that seem more serious. There are, for example, political quizzes and personality tests and even IQ tests available online for free whose results suggest that I am an introverted socialist genius. I like these better than the other tests that imply that I am a psychopath from Newark.[12] Psychologists can be quite snobbish about these online quizzes, but there is really no reason to be prejudiced about these things. It is an empirical question whether they are any good. Some of them are going to be meaningless, and others might actually have some predictive power: the difficulty is in telling them apart.

There is an entire subdiscipline within psychology called *psychometrics* dedicated to the task of understanding what we are measuring and how well we are measuring it. We have statistical techniques for checking how internally consistent a measure is, and whether any of its items are out of place. We have methods for checking whether a measure works in the same way across different groups, including cultural groups. We can also evaluate measures on how internally consistent they are as well as how stable—as opposed to fickle—they are within individuals. These are all checks for different kinds of *reliability*. There are also checks for *validity*, which assess the extent to which the measure can predict behaviors and other outcomes. A psychological measure—or Buzzfeed quiz—is good to the extent that it enjoys high levels of reliability and validity.

Everyone has heard of IQ tests: some of you may even have done some online, like I have in moments of narcissism that quickly turn to dread at the possibility of confounded expectations. If you have, then you might be disappointed—or relieved—to hear that the free online versions rarely bear any resemblance to standardized tests for general intelligence developed and evaluated by psychologists.[13] In contrast to the online tests that typically just take a few minutes to complete, the Wechsler test I mentioned earlier typically takes over an hour. It consists of 10 different tasks, including on general knowledge, vocabulary, logic, arithmetic, and pattern recognition.

The WAIS has been subjected to a lot of psychometric scrutiny since it was released in 1955. Hundreds of thousands of people have completed it or its child-friendly version, the Wechsler Intelligence Scale for Children

(WISC). The 10 WAIS subtests do measure different abilities, but it turns out that performance across tests is sufficiently intercorrelated that a single score—usually called g, for "general intelligence"—can be calculated from them. These correlations between different parts of the WAIS indicate that it is internally consistent. Furthermore, though changes do occur, for example with formal education and aging, g tends to be fairly stable within individuals, even when the test is taken years apart: this stability is sometimes called *test-retest reliability*.

The Wechsler is not the only widely used test of general intelligence: other examples include the older Stanford-Binet test, Raven's Progressive Matrices, and the Hakstian-Cattell Comprehensive Ability Battery. This means we can calculate g scores from multiple tests to see how they compare. This has not been done very frequently because it is quite time-consuming to complete a single test, let alone several of them: but when it has been done, g scores from different tests have been found to be very highly correlated with one another. This suggests that all these tests are measuring the same thing, even while having different emphases and formats. Psychometricians would say that these different tests enjoy *convergent validity*. IQ tests have also been shown to enjoy more *predictive validity* than traits like work ethic or likeability: g can be used to predict a variety of real-world outcomes, including academic success, job performance, future income, and social mobility.[14]

Intelligence is not the only trait that psychologists have tried to measure. Psychologists have been in the business of personality testing for a long time. Religiosity is arguably more like a personality trait than like a cognitive ability like intelligence, but the principles for what makes a good psychological measure are quite similar in both cases. The most widely used and researched personality tests are based on the *five-factor model* of personality, which distills personality into how conscientious, agreeable, extraverted, open to experience, and neurotic someone is. My own scores on "big five" personality tests tend to indicate that I score quite low on extraversion, high on neuroticism and openness to experience, and middlingly on agreeableness and conscientiousness. This implies that I am quite shy and anxious, but also keen to try new things, and that I am neither very cooperative nor very difficult, neither very diligent nor very lackadaisical.

As with tests for g, there are several ways to measure these five aspects of personality. The most well-regarded of these is the 240-item NEO Personality Inventory (NEO PI-R),[15] which has also enjoyed much psychometric scrutiny. Like IQ tests but to a lesser extent, big five personality tests have been found to enjoy pretty high levels of internal consistency and stability, while also being sensitive to changes over a lifetime. Combinations of personality traits are also decent predictors of various outcomes, including happiness, psychological disorders, and quality of different kinds of personal relationships.[16]

Despite their psychometric virtues, IQ and personality measurements are easily and often misunderstood, misinterpreted, and abused, often toward prejudicial ends. For example, in some jurisdictions IQ is treated as a determinant of criminal responsibility, so that anyone with an IQ score of below 70 cannot be prosecuted in the same way as anyone with an IQ score above 70. This seems reasonable enough, but in jurisdictions that still enforce the death penalty, a single IQ point can be the difference between life and death. This is a flagrant abuse of IQ tests, based on a serious misunderstanding of how they work and how precise they can be: they are certainly not precise enough for life-or-death decisions to turn on them. Similarly, personality-based explanations of conflict, especially in the workplace, can lead to complacency about improving policies and also to bias in recruitment and career progression. Personality tests do predict behavior, including conflict-related behavior, but they do so best when we consider how personality interacts with situational or environmental factors.

Perhaps the most important thing to remember about psychological measures is that they are *measures* of things, and not the things themselves. All measurements are simplifications. Even quite straightforward measures of traits like height and weight only capture certain elements of our physical stature: health professionals certainly find height and weight measurements useful, but these do not exhaustively describe our bodies. Similarly, IQ tests measure what can reasonably be called intelligence, but this does not mean that they measure everything that everyone means by the word. There are many elements and types of what we might recognize as intelligence that IQ tests do not cover, such as wisdom, common sense, creativity, and curiosity. Nor are the big five factors exhaustive of what we mean by personality, and psychologists have developed many other measures to capture specific elements of personality not covered by the five-factor model, including specific elements of *religiosity*.

Measuring religiosity

Since the 1960s, there has been an explosion in psychological measures of religiosity. We have come a long way from just asking people whether they identify with a religion or how often they attend religious services, though these are still common measures of religiosity in other social sciences. Indeed, we have come a long way from assuming that religiosity is a single trait. There is widespread recognition that there are many different aspects to and ways of being religious, and that it might be best to measure these separately rather than to try to get at a *g* or even a big five for religiosity.

We have measures not only of diverse beliefs and behaviors—beliefs about God, about the afterlife, about karma; private religious behaviors, and public ones—but also about people's religious *orientations* and *motivations*. Do they think of religion as an ongoing quest, or are they certain that they have already arrived at the absolute truth? Are they devout because they see the social and practical benefits, or because they truly believe, hook, line, and sinker? There are now hundreds of measures of different aspects of religiosity. Some of these are valid and reliable, but not all.[17] Of course, to say that there are many validated measures of religiosity is not to say that researchers always use them. In fact, very few of the studies covered in this book use validated measures. Despite the plethora of existing measures, these researchers have felt the need to construct their own measures. In most cases, they had rather good reasons to do so. Sometimes, however, I wish that they had just used a validated measure because as we shall see later on, the variability in research methods can lead to confusion when results disagree.

There is something dissatisfying about this standard method of psychological research that I have just described, even if we accept that psychologists have devised clever techniques for asking questions and interpreting answers. At least in the case of personality tests and religiosity measures, we are asking people to tell us what they are like, what they believe, how they feel. The trouble is that sometimes we don't know what we are like, what we believe, and how we feel. Our self-awareness is limited: for some people more so than for others, perhaps. To make things worse, we also have a penchant for self-deception. Sometimes, we know what we ought to think or how we ought to feel, based on societal norms or whatever, and we convince ourselves that that is what we personally think, how we personally feel. This poses an obvious problem for self-report measures. In response to this challenge, psychologists have also developed measures that do not require us to ask people directly about their thoughts and feelings.

Psychoanalysts—especially those of the Freudian persuasion—have been doing this sort of thing for decades, long before social psychologists came into the picture. They have been interpreting dreams and drawings, and catching people out for slips of the tongue, all in the effort to mine for elusive information about the workings of the unconscious. Unfortunately, these methods have all been found to be very unreliable when judged by psychometric standards. Different analysts find different things in the same dreams, drawings, and slips, which then do not predict subsequent behaviors or outcomes very well at all. They might have therapeutic value and provide a meaningful feeling of deep insight for some people, but they are not very useful as measurement tools for psychologists.

Perhaps the most obvious way to bypass self-report is to read people's *brains* directly. It would be very convenient if we could do this, but the use of neuroimaging techniques like functional magnetic resonance imaging (fMRI) for psychological measurement still lies in the realm of science fiction. This is partly because our knowledge of how the brain works is still very poor. And the more we learn, the more complex we realize brain function is. We now know, for example, that there is no "God spot" that we can measure. No specific bit of the brain "lights up" when we believe in God. Not only that, but there is probably no spot for anything. Consider, for example, the amygdala, which has been very successfully popularized as the seat of fear. The trouble is that it is a very unreliable biomarker for fear, and is also active when other emotions—disgust, sadness, even happiness—are experienced.[18] So, the fact that your amygdala is active at any given moment tells us very little about how you feel.

Neuroscientists have mostly abandoned the effort to read our minds by looking at specific spots. Instead, they are now developing ways to train computers to learn what the whole brain is doing, for instance when we are experiencing different emotions. This information can then be used to predict our emotions from new brain scans. So far, this technique performs better than just guessing randomly, but still only gets basic emotions—like fear and anger—right about a quarter of the time.[19] We have a long way to go before we will be able to measure even simple beliefs and emotions this way. Speaking to the magazine *Scientific American*, one of the pioneers of this technique, Heini Saarimäki, said, "for now I think we are still safer if you just ask people how they are feeling, rather than trying to read their brain."[20]

The techniques most widely used by experimental psychologists—including those we will meet here—exploit the relationship between time and thought. In 2011, the Nobel Prize–winning psychologist Daniel Kahneman popularized the idea in his book *Thinking, Fast and Slow* that there are interesting differences between these two types of thinking: our initial, quick gut reactions to things and our subsequent, slower rational deliberations.[21] This distinction explains a wide range of human experiences, besides the obvious one of changing our minds when we give something some critical thought. It also helps us to understand people's psychological conflicts, as well as their hypocrisies and inconsistencies.

Based on this idea, psychologists have developed ways to measure these gut reactions, our intuitions, our tacit beliefs and attitudes that might even exist *underneath* our conscious awareness. As we shall see, some of these techniques are very simple, including asking participants to respond to questions very quickly or, conversely, measuring how long they take to respond. Some are more complicated, comparing response times between different questions or different versions of a task. These sorts of measures have recently percolated into public discourse, as part of our current conversations about *implicit bias*. Employees of many governments and multinational corporations have been encouraged to complete *Implicit Association Tests* (IATs) to assess their implicit racism, for example, even though psychologists are still conducting research to understand the benefits and limitations of tasks like the IAT for psychological measurement. Bear this in mind, as we encounter time-based measures in the experiments we are looking at.

Can psychologists study religion?

We have spent a lot of this chapter thinking about measurement, which I have been advised is a pretty good way to bore readers to death. But issues of measurement are critically important, because our ability to study religion scientifically turns on our ability to measure it. Measurement is the foundation of every science, from physics to psychology. It is only when we have a good method of measurement—a reliable and valid one—that we can begin to ask more substantive questions, including questions about causes and effects. This is true whether we are talking about correlational research like Francis Galton's or experimental research like the Great Prayer Experiment.

Once we have a good method of measurement, we are more than halfway toward being able to discover all kinds of interesting things. We can, for example, run any number of correlational studies, much more rigorous than Galton's. We might want to know whether IQ predicts religiosity, for example: whether smarter people are less likely to be religious, perhaps. Equipped with the WAIS and a good measure of religiosity, we can soon begin to collect data to answer our question (for more on this, see Chapter 2). Or we might want to know whether different personality traits predict religiosity: again, equipped with the NEO-PI-R and a good measure of religiosity, we can embark on a research project.

Similarly, we might wonder whether certain experiences—say psychedelic experiences or traumatic experiences or experiences of awe or of the fear of death (see Chapter 8)—can lead directly to people becoming more religious, or less so. This requires something more than a good measure of religiosity: we would also need a way to stimulate those experiences in people, to see if they make a difference to their religiosity. But still, measurement is necessary.

And so this extended introduction to psychological measurement—and to the psychological measurement of religiosity in particular—is a way of saying, tentatively, "yes," to the question about whether psychologists can study religion. Psychologists have developed various ways of measurement various aspects of religiosity, and continue to do so.

Experimenting with religion

Now, a brief word about how I picked the seven experiments explored in the rest of the book. My first criterion was simply that they had to be experiments in which some aspect of religiosity is measured. This ruled out most of the existing psychological studies about religion, which tend be correlational in design. It also ruled out the large body of experimental research on religion usually described as *religious priming* research. In these studies, participants are reminded about religion, for example by showing them words like "god" and "church" or by having them reflect momentarily about their religious beliefs: they are then observed performing some other task, through which their honesty or generosity or cooperativeness or some other such behavior can be measured. Finally, I wanted to be able to talk to the original authors of each study, and this sadly ruled out one of the most awesome psychology experiments of all time, the Marsh Chapel Experiment, sometimes called the Good Friday Experiment.[22] Walter Pahnke performed this experiment as his doctoral research, but he died in 1971, predeceasing his doctoral advisor Timothy Leary, who died in 1996.

Just before a two-and-a-half-hour Good Friday service at Boston University's Marsh Chapel in 1962, 20 seminarians were given a white pill each. Ten of the pills contained psilocybin, an extract of magic mushrooms; the other 10 contained a placebo, vitamin B3. None of them knew which pill they had been given at first, but it did not take long before it became pretty obvious. All 20 students were interviewed and given a questionnaire about their experiences right after the service, as well as in the following days, and finally six months later. The differences between the experiences of the two groups of students were so obvious that they barely required statistical analysis.

Compared to the students who received the placebo, those who had taken psilocybin had intense experiences that they described as transcendent, paradoxical, and ineffable. They lost their sense of individuality, and gained a sense of being united with "ultimate reality." They lost their sense of time, and even space. They experienced awe and wonder. They felt profoundly happy, even ecstatic, and sometimes expressed this joy in spiritual terms. But—and this is rarely mentioned in descriptions of the Good Friday Experiment— those who had taken psychedelics were no more likely than those who had received placebos to experience the presence of God or intimacy with God; they were not more likely to experience feelings of sacredness or holiness or reverence. In other words, depending on how we define and measure "spirituality" or "religiosity," we might come away with a variety of conclusions about the effects of psychedelics.[23]

None of the experiments we will now look at were as sensational as this one, but they are arguably more relevant to understanding normal everyday religion as most of us know it, without intense mystical experience and unaided by psychedelic drugs.[24] They cover familiar religious themes: belief in and about gods old and new, belief in creation or design in the natural world, belief in the soul and its survival after death, and belief in the efficacy of rituals. These are the things that religious traditions have in common, from the so-called world religions like Christianity and Buddhism to the traditions that preceded them that we now know somewhat condescendingly as myths, whether Greco-Roman, Egyptian, Canaanite, or Chinese, to the new religious movements that emerge every so often with great enthusiasm, politically incorrectly referred to as cults by disapproving snobs with their own ideological or theological axes to grind.

In each case, the experimenters want to understand where in our minds religion comes from. To do so they have to dig deep into our minds and our religious traditions that have, for better or worse, with greater or lesser success, built their theological edifices on fertile psychological ground, if the historical and cultural ubiquity of religion is any indication. Whether they manage to do so, I leave up to you to judge.

2

Does thinking cause atheism?

Design: Between-subjects
Manipulate: Analytic thinking v. control
- Thinker v. Discobolus
Measure: Belief in God
- self-report

In the summer of 1880, the then relatively unknown sculptor Auguste Rodin was commissioned to create a set of bronze doors for Paris's planned Musée des Arts Decoratifs. As his source material, he chose Dante's *Inferno*, the first part of *The Divine Comedy*, his epic poem about a soul's journey to the after-life. "Inferno" is Italian for Hell, and the doors were to represent its gates. How the architects felt about their entrance being the gates of Hell, I do not know. In any case, the museum itself was never built, and the doors were never cast in the intended bronze during Rodin's lifetime. Far from languishing away in the artist's file drawer, however, *The Gates of Hell* became the source of many of Rodin's most famous works, including his most famous free-standing sculpture, *The Thinker*, designed to perch just above the doors.

You might be familiar with the sculpture in question: a man is seated, bent forward—almost curled up—right elbow planted into left thigh, his head lowered onto the back of an open hand, his knuckles in his teeth. The cliché is that he is pensive, lost in his thoughts. Rodin told the critic Marcel Adam in 1904 that *The Thinker* was originally meant to represent Dante himself, planning his great poem: this was certainly how it was initially interpreted by art critics. Even after the project for the museum was abandoned, the idea of *The Thinker* as a maker of things was retained: "He is not a dreamer, he is a creator."[1] The kind of thinker he had in mind was a poet, an artist: even in 1888, when *The Thinker* was first displayed detached from *The Gates of Hell*, Rodin called it *Le Poète* rather than *Le Penseur*.[2] Ever since this first exhibition in Copenhagen, *The Thinker* has been known as a work separate from *The Gates*, making his thoughts even more inscrutable. It is not clear now

Experimenting with Religion. Jonathan Jong, Oxford University Press. © Oxford University Press 2023.
DOI: 10.1093/oso/9780190875541.003.0002

who this creator is, or what creation he is contemplating. If it is no longer Dante, perhaps it is Rodin himself, surveying his masterpiece, reminiscent of Christ on his judgment seat with the whole world in the dock. When Rodin died in 1917 it was, at his request, a monumental cast of *The Thinker* that overlooked the grave, where it sits still as headstone and epitaph.

Setting aside the kind of thinker he was, it was not initially *The Thinker's* intellect that captured the imagination of the art establishment but his physique: his sharply defined muscles are tense, clenched as if ready for sudden motion. The coexistence in the same subject of brains and brawn, contemplation and action, was controversial at the time, with some praising what they saw as a message of social change and others criticizing what they saw as a lack of nobility and decorum. But it would not be long before attention turned to his thoughts, their unknowability allowing us to project our interests onto him. Over the decades, images of *The Thinker* have been used to represent all kinds of things and to advertise all kinds of products, from breakfast cereal to vodka to toilets. They also grace countless posters and course books for undergraduate courses in philosophy. Since 1931, a six-foot-tall bronze cast of Rodin's *Thinker* has occupied the lawn outside Columbia University's Philosophy Hall.

Will Gervais knew none of this as he was designing his experiment, as a doctoral student in Vancouver, Canada. All he wanted was something that reminded people of thinking: thinking *analytically* in particular. If he could find a way to put people into that frame of mind, he could then see if that had any effect on their religious beliefs. In particular, Will wanted to see if analytic thinking would *reduce* religious beliefs. So, he ran an experiment to see whether merely looking at pictures of *The Thinker* could make people less religious.

Religion, intelligence, and thinking style

Will is now at Brunel University, just outside of London, but he grew up in Colorado and started off at the University of Denver studying environmental science and biology. By the time he was ready for graduate school, however, he had decided to investigate the ways in which biological and cultural evolution come together to shape the way human beings think and behave. So, off he went to the University of British Columbia to work with Ara Norenzayan, who by then had already begun taking this biocultural evolutionary approach to the study of religion.

The early- and mid-2000s—before Will arrived in Vancouver—saw the publication of a slew of books about the evolutionary and psychological underpinnings of religion. At that time, it seemed to Will that researchers were all trying to explain the pervasiveness of religion. Religion is one of those culturally universal phenomena, like language and music, and people were interested in figuring out how it got that way. But Will wanted to know why some people *weren't* religious: after all, absence is as much in need of explanation as ubiquity.

One common hypothesis is based on the idea that human beings are religious by default. This does not necessarily mean that we are "hardwired" to believe in gods by our genetic makeup or our neurochemistry; it could just mean most of us are born into cultures where religious ideas are very influential because they have, over the centuries, been woven into our social, political, and moral norms. Regardless of how this happened, religion is the status quo, and to be *non*religious is to have overridden this default. The ability and tendency to think *analytically* might be one of the things that enables people to shake off the psychological and social forces that usually make religious beliefs so compelling to so many people.

Variations on this idea have been around for a long time, but it comes into its own in the 19th century in the form of the conjecture that science would eventually displace supernatural and superstitious beliefs. This version of the theory—found most forcefully in writings of the French philosopher August Comte—construes religious beliefs as primitive attempts to explain and control natural phenomena. Given that this job is more adequately done by the natural sciences, it is inevitable that religion will decay as science and technology gain ascendancy. Throughout the 19th and 20th centuries, social scientists—including Max Weber, Émile Durkheim, and Karl Marx—all composed their own variations and elaborations on this theme.

As a prediction of demographic changes at societal levels, this hypothesis has not held up well. Despite the massive advances in science, technology, and education around the world since Comte's day, there is no strong evidence of religious decline at the global level. Whatever the effects are of scientific modernization on religiosity, it is outweighed by other factors, such as the difference in birthrates between religious and nonreligious families. There may be numerically more atheists by the year 2050 than there are now, but they will probably make up a smaller proportion of the world's population than they currently do.[3]

Still, there might be something to the psychological claim that underpins the sociological prediction. Perhaps at the *individual* level, exposure to and training in critical thinking or science might lead people to shrug off the religious beliefs with which they were brought up. There is, as it turns out, no clear and consistent relationship between educational attainment—typically measured in terms of years of formal schooling—and religiosity. In some countries, like Ecuador and Serbia, people with no religious affiliation enjoy higher levels of education. In other countries, like Malaysia and Tanzania, people who are religiously affiliated enjoy higher levels of education; in yet other countries, like the United States, United Kingdom, Russia, and China, there isn't much difference either way.[4]

Even though patterns within countries are varied, countries with higher average levels of educational attainment do tend to be home to higher proportions of nonreligious people: or, as social scientists say, there is a *negative correlation* between national educational level and national religiosity. This might suggest that education undermines religion, but perhaps the pattern is coincidental. Countries with high average educational attainment are also wealthier, safer, and more stable than those of lower average educational attainment, and all of these different traits are also associated with decreased religiosity.[5] We cannot say from correlations alone which of these variables— if any—*cause* a decline in religiosity.

Perhaps general education level is too broad a factor to examine in any case. Sociologists have also looked to see if professional scientists tend to be less religious than the general population, and they are, though there is some cross-cultural variation here too: in Hong Kong and Taiwan, for example, scientists seem to be *more* religious than other people.[6] Without knowing more about how professional scientists differ from other people—in terms of their upbringing, their socioeconomic situation, their personality, all of which might contribute to someone's religiosity—it is difficult to know why this gap exists between scientists and nonscientists. This comparison is too blunt a tool for our purposes. If we want to know whether there are any interesting *psychological* differences between religious and nonreligious people, we have to measure them as directly as possible.

Assuming you were sufficiently convinced earlier that IQ tests are not completely meaningless and that they measure, albeit imperfectly, general cognitive ability, they are as good a place as any to begin. Previous research suggests that being very intelligent predicts upward social mobility[7]: maybe the ability to transcend our socioeconomic backgrounds also enables us to push back against any predispositions we might have toward religious belief. Fortunately for us, there is a substantial body of evidence on this, though the data are mostly from the United States and other Western countries.

Miron Zuckerman, a psychologist at the University of Rochester, and his colleagues Jordan Silberman and Judith Hall recently gathered together 63 studies involving over 70,000 individuals and estimated from them that their IQ was negatively correlated to religious belief.[8] The estimated strength of the correlation was around −0.2 to −0.25. Correlations can vary between −1 and 1, which imply *perfect* negative and positive relationships respectively; a correlation strength of 0 means that the two variables are unrelated.

By way of comparison with another IQ-related correlation, an earlier analysis based on 31 samples involving over 58,000 individuals—again, mostly from the United States and other Western countries—estimated the positive correlation between youth IQ and future income at 0.21.[9] This correlation strength is just about average in these kinds of meta-analyses in psychology, and is larger than many other correlations that we take for granted.[10] For example, we are widely advised to take aspirin when we suspect that we are having a heart attack, but the correlation between taking aspirin and reduced risk of death in this situation is a measly 0.02, 10 times weaker than the IQ–religiosity relationship.[11]

One interpretation offered by Zuckerman and colleagues of their findings is the one we have been considering, and which piqued Will Gervais's interest. In their paper, Zuckerman, Silberman, and Hall write, "we propose that more intelligent people tend to think analytically and that analytic thinking leads to lower religiosity."[12] Cognitive psychologists mean something quite specific when they talk about *analytic* thinking. Being analytic is not quite the same as being intelligent: it is a cognitive *style* rather than purely a cognitive ability, though of course ability does come into it. Roughly speaking, to think analytically is to think deliberately, and not to rely on our unexamined immediate intuitions.[13]

As it is distinct from intelligence, analytic thinking is not measured with an IQ test but with the Cognitive Reflection Test (CRT)[14] or a questionnaire like the Rational-Experiential Inventory (REI).[15] The REI is basically a self-report personality test: it asks questions about our subjective preferences, for which there are no "right" or "wrong" answers. In contrast, the CRT is much more of an objective *test* in the same vein as an IQ test. However, it is a test that most people would be able to pass, as long as they paused to think instead of going with their initial impression.

Here's an example, from cognitive scientist Shane Frederick's original paper on the CRT:

> A bat and a ball cost $1.10 in total. The bat costs $1.00 more than the ball. How much does the ball cost?

The intuitive response—which comes first to mind for most people—is 10 cents. But, of course, this is wrong: if the ball cost 10 cents and the bat costs $1 more, it would cost $1.10, which would make the total cost $1.20 rather than $1.10. The correct answer has to be 5 cents, which means that the bat costs $1.05, bringing the total to the correct $1.10.

The most obvious problem with this task is that it looks like a measure of mathematical ability and is in fact correlated with measures of numerical ability.[16] But not very much mathematical skill is required to arrive at the correct answer: all it takes is simple addition and subtraction.[17] As long as people stop and think, they should get it right. That's the idea, anyway. We do not yet know very much about *how* people think through the test. Do they actually suppress the intuitive response before arriving at the correct answer via deliberation? Does deliberation usually lead to the correct answer? Some recent research suggests that this picture is mistaken, and that some people are just intuitively better at these tasks.[18] If so, then the CRT is a measure of cognitive ability after all, rather than of cognitive style. Psychological measurement is hard.

For the sake of the argument, let us assume that the CRT is an adequate measure of analytic thinking as cognitive psychologists understand it. Having already seen that there is a negative correlation between IQ and religiosity, we might want to know if CRT scores are also negatively associated with religiosity.[19] Gordon Pennycook and colleagues recently gathered together 31 different studies involving over 15,000 participants—mostly from the United States and Canada—and estimated the correlation to be −0.18, just a little lower than Zuckerman's estimation of the intelligence-religiosity link.[20]

The Rodin experiment

Maybe it shouldn't, but it always surprises me how different teams of researchers seem to independently come up with very similar ideas at the same time. Before 2012, there was pretty much no published research on analytic thinking and religiosity. Some studies on scientists' religious beliefs and the intelligence–religiosity correlation were available, but nothing with the CRT. In 2012, three different teams—led by Amitai Shenhav at Harvard, Gordon Pennycook at the University of Waterloo, and Will Gervais at the University of British Columbia, all doctoral students at the time—published papers reporting CRT–religiosity correlations. Shenhav's paper was published first, while Will and his doctoral supervisor Ara were revising their paper based on reviewers' feedback. Pennycook's came next, followed by Will and Ara's just a few weeks later, in the journal *Science*, one of the world's most prestigious scientific periodicals, founded in 1880 with the financial backing of Thomas Edison and later Alexander Graham Bell.

It is Will's *experiments* that interest me most, rather than the correlational findings his paper shared in common with the others. He wanted to manipulate people's thinking style—to put them temporarily in an analytic frame of mind—to see if that would reduce their religious beliefs. It turns out that there were a few ways that he could have gone about this: cognitive styles seem easier to shift than, say, general intelligence. Education can increase IQ test performance—by 1 to 5 points for each additional year of schooling[21]—but manipulating it in a laboratory is quite a different proposition.

He thinks he got the idea of using Rodin's *Thinker* when an image of it showed up on someone else's presentation about analytic and intuitive thinking. Scientific inspiration is often banal. But the Rodin study wasn't the first attempt. Before this, Will had read that just presenting words in a font that is difficult to read—faded, italicized, and so forth—can put people into an analytic mindset. The idea is that reading difficult fonts is effortful, which encourages people to make the extra effort of thinking more deliberately. So, the first experiment he ran involved two groups of participants who either answered questions about their religious beliefs printed in difficult or normal font: as hypothesized, he found that participants whose questionnaires were difficult to read reported lower levels of religious belief than those whose questionnaires were printed normally.

He also ran two other studies using a *sentence unscrambling* task, in which participants are given a jumble of words that they are asked to turn into a grammatically correct sentence by dropping one of the words and rearranging the others. For example, participants may be presented with:

dog away deli ran the

which they would rearrange as

the dog ran away

by first dropping "deli." In these studies, there were two versions of the sentence unscrambling task, one of which contained words like "reason," "ponder," and "think," obviously meant to remind participants of analytic thinking; the other version did not contain such words. Again, participants who completed the analytic version of the task subsequently reported lower levels of religiosity.

While these other studies are rather interesting in their own right, it was the Rodin experiment that grabbed me. I don't exactly know why, but it may have had something to do with Dostoevsky. In her diaries, Anna Dostoevsky recalls her husband standing before a painting in Basel by Hans Holbein the Younger: it was *The Body of the Dead Christ in the Tomb*, and the great novelist stood before it, as if stunned. He was, she recounts, both transfixed and agitated.

"A painting like that," he said to her, "can make you lose your faith."[22]

A year or so after this incident in 1867, the painting found itself as the central—iconic, if you will—object of Dostoevsky's tragic novel *The Idiot*.[23] A copy of Holbein's *Dead Christ* hangs in a house, where it is seen by the protagonist Prince Myshkin, himself a sort of Christ figure. Myshkin's reaction mirrors Dostoevksy's own: he exclaims, "That picture! A man could lose his faith looking at that picture!"

The Dead Christ makes you lose your faith because it is bleak: it depicts, in unforgiving realism, the mutilated corpse of a crucified man, claustrophobically entombed. There is no indication of who the man in the painting is *per se*. The identity of the anonymous criminal has to be imposed, from above as it were, in an inscription on the frame, borne by angels: IESVS NAZARENVS REX IVDAEORVM. Jesus lies unceremoniously on a carelessly draped slab; his face is turned slightly toward the viewer, with eyes open and glassy, mouth slightly agape. The grayish-green of putrefaction and the stiffness of rigor mortis have set in; Holbein's Christ is truly, almost hyperbolically, dead. As such, it is—Dostoevsky's readers are meant to understand—devoid of all hope, especially the hope of resurrection. In the face of Christ's hopeless deadness, there is no reason to believe in him or his God.

This is not at all how *The Thinker* is meant to work. All the same, Will's idea that looking at a work of art could make a difference to our religious beliefs reminded me of Dostoevsky's response to Holbein's painting. After Will decided on *The Thinker*, he still needed a control condition against which to compare the experimental condition. For this purpose, Myron's *Discobolus*— the discus thrower—was deemed sufficiently similar without any of the cerebral connotations of *The Thinker*. The *Discobolus* is a Greek sculpture from the 5th century BCE of an athlete just about to release his discus. At this level of description, it is a plausible candidate for playing the jock to *The Thinker*'s nerd. The irony is that it is also the less grotesquely muscular of the two, and *The Thinker*'s face is the more emotional: the material details of the sculptures do not fit the desired stereotypes well at all. But there is a world of a difference between art criticism and psychology experimental design, and maybe the finer points of the former are irrelevant for the latter.

Whether or not seeing *The Thinker* and *Discobolus* affects people's tendencies to engage in analytic thinking is, of course, an empirical question, no less than the question of whether they can affect people's religious beliefs. Before running their main study, Will and Ara ran a small—"quick and dirty," as Will describes it—pilot study to see if they had chosen their artworks well. They had 40 participants in the pilot study, half of whom were shown pictures of *The Thinker* and the other half of whom were shown pictures of *Discobolus*. Rather than using the CRT as a measure of analytic thinking, they showed the participants a series of simple arguments, which they had to judge as *valid* or not. In formal logic, the validity of an argument has nothing to do with whether its conclusion is true or false: an argument is valid if its conclusion—whatever it may be—follows from its premises. Here's an example using some nonsense words:

Premise 1: All greebles are yalish.
Premise 2: Isabel is a greeble.
Conclusion: Isabel is yalish.[24]

This argument is valid. Assuming that both premises are true, the conclusion must also be true. Consider another argument that looks very similar:

Premise 1: All greebles are yalish.
Premise 2: Bob is yalish.
Conclusion: Bob is a greeble.

This argument is invalid, because even if both premises were true, this does not guarantee that the conclusion is: for example, perhaps yalishness is a very common trait shared by different species including greebles, ploks, and glips, and Bob happens to be a yalish glip. Crucially, even if the argument is invalid, its conclusion might still be true. Bob could, in fact, be a greeble, even though this argument fails to demonstrate that. Here's an example of an invalid argument whose conclusion happens to be true:

> Premise 1: All humans are mortal.
> Premise 2: Socrates is mortal.
> Conclusion: Socrates is a human.

Socrates is—or *was*, in any case—human, but that conclusion does not follow from the argument: being mortal is, as we imagined being yalish to be, a trait common to all kinds of creatures. Simply knowing that humans are mortal and that Socrates is too does not infallibly tell us that Socrates is a human: he could be a giraffe, since they are also mortal.

This is the sort of thing Will and Ara showed to their participants. Some of the arguments they provided were valid, but had implausible conclusions: others were invalid, but had plausible conclusions. Previous research had shown that people's ability to correctly evaluate the validity of an argument is influenced by whether they believe the conclusion: this is called the *belief bias*.[25] When people do believe the conclusion of an argument, they often wrongly judge an invalid argument to be valid; and when they don't believe the conclusion, they often wrongly judge a valid argument to be invalid. Take, for example, this argument that Will and Ara used:

> Premise 1: All things that are made of plants are good for the health.
> Premise 2: All cigarettes are things that are made of plants.
> Conclusion: All cigarettes are good for the health.

Most people disbelieve the conclusion, and as a result, we often judge this argument to be *invalid*, even though the premises do guarantee the conclusion. The trouble with the argument is not that it is invalid but that at least the first premise is false. It's not true that all plant-based materials are good for our health: but if both premises *were* true, the conclusion—as unpalatable as it might be to our sensibilities—would be too. The falsity of the conclusion distracts us from being able to recognize this, until we stop and think about it carefully. In other words, overcoming the belief bias seems to rely on the same cognitive process as the CRT; researchers do generally find that the two tasks are highly correlated.[26]

As they had hoped, participants who viewed images of *The Thinker* performed better at this reasoning task than those who viewed images of *Discobolus*. This allowed them to carry on to the main experiment, which had a very similar setup to the pilot. It wasn't even a much larger study, with a total of 57 participants, all undergraduate students, as is still so typical in psychology experiments. The students were first told that they were going to participate in several different studies. This was to discourage them from connecting the artwork to the later question about religiosity. Will and Ara even asked participants at the end of the study if they could guess what it was actually about: some people could, and their data were removed from the analyses.

To throw participants off the scent, the artwork task was falsely described as a study about memory: they were to look at four images for 30 seconds, ostensibly for a memory test later. Half of the participants saw four images of *The Thinker* whereas the other half saw four images of *Discobolus*.[27] After this, participants filled in a questionnaire that asked for basic demographic information about themselves, like their age and gender; again, very typical of psychology studies. Among these questions was one about whether they believed in God. Participants rated their belief in God from 0 to 100, where 0 meant "God definitely does not exist" and 100 meant "God definitely exists."

As with their other experiments in this paper, Will and Ara found here that participants who viewed images of *The Thinker*—for all of two minutes—reported lower belief in God than those who viewed *Discobolus*. Especially considering the simplicity and brevity of the manipulation, the effect was quite large: on average, participants who viewed *Discobolus* rated their belief in God at about 60 out of 100, whereas those who viewed *The Thinker* rated their belief in God at about 40. Assuming that the midpoint of the scale—50—implies the border between disbelief and belief, this simple experimental manipulation seems to have turned believers into skeptics.

This study made the news. *New Scientist* covered it; *Scientific American* featured it twice; *Mother Jones*—not usually known for its scientific content— called the *Thinker* study "one amazing experiment."[28] As I am writing this, it is still mentioned favorably in a Wikipedia entry on religion and intelligence. Talking to *Scientific American*, Joshua Greene—a psychologist at Harvard and coauthor of Shenhav's paper—lauded it for its rigor, especially for showing the same effect using different experimental methods. At the time, I shared this positive assessment of the paper, and was pleased to see work in my field featured in so prestigious a publication.

The replication crisis in social psychology

There was a crisis brewing while Will, Amitai Shenhav, Gordon Pennycook, and I were in graduate school. The first major sign that something was wrong with the field dropped in August 2010: the Harvard evolutionary biologist and cognitive scientist Marc Hauser was found guilty of perpetrating scientific fraud, of fabricating data. He was widely known for his work on moral decision-making, and the irony of this was not lost on us. A year later, Diederik Stapel, a social psychologist at Tilburg University was suspended, also for fabricating and otherwise manipulating data. Besides these two incidents, two papers were published that caused a different kind of furor, not over outright dishonesty but over *questionable research practices*, now dubbed QRPs.

By the end of 2010, there was draft of a paper circulating, in which Daryl Bem, a prominent social psychologist at Cornell, claimed to have found evidence for extrasensory perception: the paper reported nine experiments involving over 1,000 participants, which found that people—regular people, to the extent that Cornell undergraduates are regular people—could "feel" if not quite *see* into the future. The paper was eventually published in the *Journal of Personality and Social Psychology* (JPSP), a top-tier psychology journal. This kicked up all kinds of dust. Criticisms of Bem's methods came furiously, but very soon, psychologists began noticing that Bem wasn't really doing anything unusually egregious. His statistical practices were normal, in the sense that they were how psychologists typically ran studies and analyzed data. This led to widespread anxiety about how many of our other findings published in respected journals were bunk, driven more by shoddy practices rather than by reality. Ideas for how to reform the field were exchanged with great urgency and fervor, both in the pages of academic journals and more informally among friends and collaborators: we need much larger samples, psychologists declared, and better statistical techniques, and open access to raw data, and more efforts to replicate findings.[29]

The calls to replicate findings were quickly answered. In October 2011,[30] Brian Nosek was just beginning the effort that would become the Centre for Open Science, now the beating heart of efforts to improve science from within. By August 2012, he had persuaded dozens of researchers to volunteer to re-run other people's experiments, reported in three important psychology journals, including JPSP: they ended up attempting to replicate a hundred studies.[31]

While Nosek was building up this movement, Stéphane Doyen—then a graduate student in Belgium, now a data scientist for a management consultancy—published a failed replication of a single study, incidentally also published in JPSP, but it was one of the most beloved and widely cited experiments in social psychology[32]: John Bargh's 1996 study, showing that just reading words associated with old age (e.g., gray, retired, ancient) made participants walk more slowly.[33] This study was a classic in the field. Not only had it been cited thousands of times, but social psychologists regularly taught it to their students. It was the paradigmatic example of how our behaviors and attitudes can easily be manipulated, or *primed*, simply using words and pictures. Very quickly, it became the darling of marketing executives as well as conspiracy theorists obsessed with subliminal priming. And now, Doyen was showing that Bargh's experiment was a fluke.

These events and the burgeoning movement of self-examination and efforts to improve affected Will too. Looking back to his time at graduate school, he recalls that he hadn't seriously expected those subtle primes to shift people's religious beliefs. "Even at the time it seemed like a silly idea, really," he admitted to me. His findings came to him as a pleasant surprise, though not—at the time—as a cause for suspicion. The paper's acceptance by *Science* provided another cause for confidence. But this confidence soon waned as Will learned more about QRPs, and how to recognize the fingerprints of shoddy research. His studies on analytic thinking and religion looked guilty as sin. He had also since tried to do more work with the sentence unscrambling task and kept finding no effects, once he applied the more rigorous standards that he had picked up since graduate school. It occurred to him to try to replicate the Rodin study himself, but never prioritized it. Then, in May 2014, he received an email from an undergraduate student Clinton Sanchez and his professor Robert Calin-Jageman.

Teaching by replicating

Bob Calin-Jageman studies sea slugs. But at least in my neck of the woods, that's not what he's known for. What he's best known for are his careful attempts to replicate social psychology studies. He has only replicated about a half a dozen social psychological studies to date, but they are each shining exemplars of how to go about this. It's not just the studies themselves that I admire, but the entire process he has constructed—his team always contacts the original authors to obtain the original materials, they always first pitch the paper to the journal that published the original study. It is easy to accuse academics who spend a lot of time publishing failed replications of other people's work of being persecutory parasites, but not Bob.

It all started in 2010 or so, not long after he joined the psychology faculty at Dominican University in Illinois and was asked to coteach the research methods and statistics class there. For this class, undergraduates had to come up with research ideas and run studies to test them. They were learning by doing, which is no bad thing. As you might expect, this is quite a lot to ask of an undergraduate student. The knowledge and skills required to consult a research literature, define a testable hypothesis, design a rigorous study, and run statistical analyses are usually developed in graduate school, mentored by an experienced researcher. Bob figured that a better thing for the students to do is what apprentices have been doing for centuries: learning by copying, which after all is a sort of doing. The desire to run replications studies came first from a pedagogical insight, rather than from an aim to scrutinize published research.

Bob has a list of studies, a menu of papers he has collected over the years, whose experiments are both interesting and feasible for undergraduate students at a small, teaching-oriented college without much of a research budget. The students pick a study and get in touch with the original team of researchers, out of courtesy as well as for practical help and advice. Published scientific articles are meant to contain enough methodological detail to permit others to independently replicate our work, but they rarely actually do. This makes the cooperation of the original researchers crucial for successful replication. They are not always very helpful, perhaps because replication attempts are still seen as a threat, even an accusation. Researchers worry that they are being tarred with the same brush as Hauser or Stapel or Bem or Bargh or Amy Cuddy, whose case is perhaps the most high-profile so far.

Cuddy's case is worth saying a little more about, as its effects have rippled well beyond the academy. In her TED Talk that went viral in 2012, she introduced the idea that *power posing*—standing in a manner that projects confidence, just for a couple of minutes—makes us feel more confident, and even leads us toward more reward-seeking risks. She even claimed that power posing increased testosterone levels and decreased cortisol, commonly believed to be associated with aggression and stress respectively.[34] With characteristic efficiency, the business world leapt onto this bandwagon, and why wouldn't they? Power posing was a simple, quick, and seemingly scientific route to success, to the extent that great success required great risk-taking. And then, in 2015, Cuddy's findings failed to replicate: power posing made participants *feel* more confident, but did not affect their behavior or their hormone levels.[35] The news spread rapidly within the field, and Cuddy's name became a by-word for QRPs almost overnight: the story of her downfall was even featured in the *New York Times Magazine*.[36]

To be sure, failures to replicate have cost people their reputations, if not necessarily their careers: Bargh is still at Yale and Cuddy is still at Harvard, albeit in a different position. But I believe Bob when he tells me that it isn't his intention to debunk studies, less still to ruin academic careers. He does not choose studies that he or his students suspect might fail to replicate. In fact, in the early years, when he began noticing that his students were more often than not failing to replicate published results, he wondered whether it was because they lacked the skills to do so. Perhaps they had failed to match the methodologies properly, or conversely, failed to adapt the study sufficiently for their specific context. People sometimes say that replicating a study is like following a recipe that a brilliant chef has prepared: all the creative work has already been done, as it were.

"Baloney," Bob says.

Replication requires translation, sometimes even literally if the original study was conducted in a different language. But there are subtle and surprising tweaks that can be made too, and it is not always obvious which modifications are necessary. Bob's first published replication study was about whether people perform better at golf when they believe that the golf ball they have been given is *lucky*. The original study was conducted in Germany, and it turns out that American students are considerably better at golf than German students. So, they had to adjust the task to make it more difficult: otherwise everyone would just perform maximally well regardless of whether their ball was deemed lucky.[37]

Replicating Rodin

Like all studies, the Rodin experiment needed to be translated to be replicated. In this case, Bob worried about the religious composition of his university: Dominican University, affiliated with the Sinsinawa Dominican Sisters, is a Catholic university, and is much more religious than the University of British Columbia. He did not know if this would make a big difference, but just in case, he also recruited participants online and from two other nearby colleges, a public community college as well as private Lutheran university. Everything else could remain the same. As is common practice in replication studies, this one also multiplied the number of participants: Bob ended up with 411 participants, more than seven times Will and Ara's original sample. The number of participants is important because the statistical techniques psychologists and other social scientists use are more reliable when there is more data. If Bob's team failed to replicate the result, it would neither be for lack of trying nor lack of statistical power.

Bob does not remember how Will's paper first got on his list, but it is not surprising that it did. The paper was a sensation and met all of Bob's criteria: it was an exciting result, the design was simple, the materials were free as soon as Will handed over the images he used of *The Thinker* and *Discobolus*. It was Bob's undergraduate student Clinton Sanchez who picked it off the list. Clinton was always interested in religion and had already completed a research project on religiosity and well-being. This was right up his alley, and so he got in touch with Will, hopeful for his cooperation. Will remembers his initial anxiety upon receiving Clinton's email: after all, he had already begun to doubt the replicability of this—still his most well-cited—study. By Bob's account, however, Will's anxiety did not turn into obstruction: Will has, he says, been unusually "energetic, collaborative, unthreatened, and willing to change his beliefs based on the data."

You will, at this point, not be shocked to discover that the finding did not replicate. The next step was to try to publish. This should have been easy. They failed to replicate a widely praised and well-cited study, published in *Science*, one of the most important scientific journals in the world: and they enjoyed Will's support and endorsement. Indeed, *Science* should have jumped at the opportunity to set the record straight. Clinton, Bob, and their collaborators thought so too, and submitted their paper there first. What they received instead was an impersonal rejection letter stating that their paper "was not given a high priority rating." This gave Bob a rare opportunity to send a sharp retort to the venerable journal. "I guess science as a whole is self-correcting, but *Science* the journal is not," he quipped.

After *Science*, they tried two other venues, neither of which even sent the paper out for review: finally, the open-access journal *PLOS One* had a proper look at it. It was assigned to Michiel van Elk, also a psychologist of religion, based at the University of Amsterdam, who has since developed a serious interest in replication research. The paper was independently reviewed as usual, but in addition to that, Michiel sent it to Will for a final look. Will had no objections, and so it was published in February 2017, seven years after the original studies were run in Vancouver, five years after the *Science* paper came out, three years after Clinton first contacted Will. Science as a whole may be self-correcting, as Bob says, but the corrections do not come quickly. As Will notes in a blog post about the experience, researchers who replicate other people's work are out for quick and easy notoriety are kidding themselves.[38]

Clinton and Bob's was the first but is no longer the only failed replication of Will and Ara's study. In August 2018, the Rodin study was included among the 21 studies a team of researchers selected for attempted replication as part of a move to check the social and psychological research published in the two most prestigious science journals *Science* and *Nature*. Overall, they found that two-thirds of the results were replicable, but Will and Ara's failed the test.[39] No one has yet directly re-run the other main experiments they reported, but these are not likely to replicate either. Studies with much larger samples than Will and Ara's pilot tests have since found that neither the font manipulation nor the sentence unscrambling task had any effect on performance on the Cognitive Reflection Test.[40]

What does this mean for the research question at hand? Does analytic thinking reduce religious belief? Correlational studies like Gordon Pennycook's suggest that there is a relationship at the level of traits: people who are more prone to analytic thinking are less religious, though there might be some cross-cultural variation here too.[41] Will recently led an effort to collect data from 13 countries, and although their overall findings were similar to Gordon Pennycook's, the strength of the relationship varied widely across countries: he describes the overall correlation as being "in the super tiny range." But—as the social scientist's mantra goes—correlation does not entail causation, and Will's experimental tests of the causal hypothesis have proven unreliable. He still thinks that it is possible to shift people's religious beliefs—just a little, for just a moment—by putting them in an analytic frame of mind: he just doesn't think that he managed to do it.

Shenhav Amitai's paper also included an experimental manipulation of cognitive styles, and with a larger sample too: over 350 participants, across four conditions. Participants were asked to either recall a time when they followed their "first instinct" or when they used "careful reasoning." Furthermore, half of each group was asked to think of a time when the strategy led to success, while the other group was asked to think of a time when that strategy failed. The manipulation was obviously designed to shift participants' attitudes toward intuitive or analytic thinking. Analogous to Will and Ara's findings, they found that making people more favorably disposed toward intuitive thinking—or more negatively disposed toward analytic thinking—increased participants' belief in God. When I spoke to him, Will thought that it had a better chance of working than his own efforts, but there has since also been at least one failed replication of this study.[42]

Experimenting with religion, redux

Admittedly, a debunked study is an odd way to start a book about experimental research about religion. That may be, but I hope it is also a way for us to begin our journey sober. We will be looking at several more experiments throughout the book and retreading some of the same ground again about the challenges of measurement and manipulation, the importance of considering cultural context, and so forth. But very few of the studies that we will be looking at have undergone the rigorous reexamination that the Rodin study has. Replication research is still rare in general, and almost entirely nonexistent in psychology. This is hardly surprising, given how much we—not just scientists, but members of the general public too—fetishize novelty and originality over the rigorous examination of previous research. As such, all these studies have to be treated as preliminary results, subject to revision and even falsification: it is entirely possible that some of these studies will have been debunked by the time this book goes to print. It turns out that the work we will be looking at is *experimental* in two senses: the technical scientific sense and the colloquial sense that connotes novelty, tentativeness, provisionality.

This sense of provisionality is fitting. Psychology is a very new science and maybe not even quite a science yet, in the way that physics, chemistry, and biology might be. Or maybe thinking about so young and seemingly uncertain a science can teach us to think about the older more established sciences anew, which are after all also always evolving and therefore also young in parts. Take, for example, neuroscience and astrophysics, whose methods have come a long way since Galen was vivisecting animals to learn what different nerves did and Tycho Brahe was tracking the movement of Mars with his naked eye. Research methods have certainly become more powerful—we now have fMRI machines and radio telescopes—but with power comes complexity, and with complexity comes room for error and misunderstanding.

It is one thing to make inferences about recurrent laryngeal nerves when we can directly observe that severing them renders a mammal mute. It is quite another matter to figure out what an fMRI machine is telling us when our understanding of how these machines work is necessarily more limited than our ability to comprehend how a scalpel does. Similarly, it is one thing to *look* at a planet's motion, even through an optical telescope, which we know works by refracting light. It is another thing altogether to interpret the output of radio telescope arrays, which sometimes comprise dozens of satellite dishes laid out across miles of desert.

In April 2019, the first-ever image of a black hole was released: but it is not as though someone went to the supergiant elliptical galaxy Messier 87 with a Nikon. It is 16.4 million parsecs away and would take 54 million years to travel there at the speed of light. The image was constructed from data collected by the Event Horizon Telescope, which is made up of multiple telescope arrays located all around the world from Hawaii to the South Pole: these telescopes collected five petabytes—that is, five million gigabytes—worth of data.

The mathematics required to make any sense of astronomical data or, for that matter, the raw output of an fMRI machine is beyond any human being's ability to perform by hand. We are heavily reliant on algorithms for this, and often our algorithms are faulty. In 2016, a team of researchers found errors in commonly used fMRI analysis software that could invalidate thousands of published findings.[43] As techniques like these become increasingly common and easy to use, researchers tend to become complacent about learning exactly how they work, which in turn allows errors to creep in. This is a reminder that even the most technically sophisticated science is conducted by human beings, with all our ingenuity and diligence as well as our cognitive limitations and emotional foibles, and the social and institutional pressures that buffet us.

The point of this book is not to teach you a set of indubitable *facts* about human psychology as regards religion. Rather, it is to tell stories about how certain people's curiosities have led them to this kind of research, and to provide a sense of what it is like to do it, to use these tools that we have been grateful to inherit—the experimental method, psychometric instruments, cognitive tasks, statistics—as a means of understanding this thing: the belief in gods and ghosts and heavens and hells.

3

Are children creationists?

Design: Within-subjects
Manipulate:
1. Object type
- animal v. nonliving natural object
2. Explanation type
- teleological v. nonteleological
Measure: Preference

My part in this story begins in the winter of 2004, that is to say June, because we are in Dunedin, on the east coast of the South Island of Aotearoa New Zealand, just under 5,000 miles away from home on the northwestern tip of Borneo. Having successfully wrestled with the university bureaucracy to get myself enrolled as a psychology major, I retreated to the comfort and warmth of the central library. I had never seen so many books in my life: just rows upon rows of austere metal shelving holding rows upon rows of the true wealth of the university. As chance would have it, the stairs terminated right next to the Class B category of books, which in the Library of Congress Classification system denotes "Philosophy, Psychology, Religion." The rest of the day is now a blur to me, of walking up and down and up and down the corridors of books, occasionally climbing on stools to peer more closely at titles I could not see on the top shelf. Eventually, I found myself among academic journals, a genre with which I was hitherto unfamiliar. It is funny to think that my life may have turned out very differently, had the replacement of printed journals by digital versions been more advanced at the time.

The first journal that caught my eye was the May 2004 edition of *Psychological Science*, the most recent on the shelf. It is, as I would discover later, the flagship periodical of the Association for Psychological Science, one of psychology's two main professional organizations. It sounded just like the sort of thing a fresh-faced psychology major ought to be reading. Immediately, two articles in the issue leapt out at me. One was called *Do dogs*

Experimenting with Religion. Jonathan Jong, Oxford University Press. © Oxford University Press 2023.
DOI: 10.1093/oso/9780190875541.003.0003

resemble their owners?,[1] which would end up being the second academic article I had ever read (Spoiler: Yes, if the dog is a purebred.). The other was by Deborah Kelemen, a developmental psychologist at Boston University, who posed a slightly different question: *Are children "intuitive theists"?*[2] It seemed too good to be true, like a sign from God that I was in the right place, enrolled in the right undergraduate program. My church leaders back home in Malaysia had been skeptical: they would have preferred me to study theology as preparation for a career in the church. Instead, I had decided that a degree in psychology would be better training for pastoral ministry. But look, here was a psychologist studying religion! The thought of this combination had never occurred to me. I devoured the article in great excitement, only half comprehending what I was reading.

As I quickly discovered despite my partial understanding, Deb's paper is not really about *theism*, if by that you mean what philosophers and theologians tend to mean, which is belief in God-with-a-capital-G. Christianity, Judaism, and Islam do have different ideas about God, but they also share a common heritage, influenced by each other and by the writings of Plato and Aristotle. In deliberate contrast to the gods of the so-called pagan myths—Greek, Roman, Norse, and the rest—God is the utterly transcendent creator of all things on whom all things depend, beyond time and space, beyond all limits, including of knowledge and power. Deb was not arguing that children intuitively grasp this concept of God, let alone believe it: frankly, most adults don't either, as we shall see in later chapters. The claim is much humbler, which is not to say that it is less interesting: it is that children are predisposed to think of the world—including the natural world—as *designed*.

Design in the mind

For something to be designed is simply for it to have been intentionally made, typically with some function in mind, even if that function is merely to be ornamental and even if that function is not very successfully fulfilled. From croissants to computers, pavements to paintings, windows to wristwatches, we are surrounded by designed objects that exist for purposes intended by artists and architects, programmers and pastry chefs. But not everything is designed. Some things are incidental byproducts of design, such as manufacturing waste. Some things happen by accident, such as when someone slams a window shut so hard that the glass smashes: the shards might make a pretty pattern on the ground, but no one designed that pattern, even if the aggressive handling of the window was deliberate.

The natural world is also full of things that are, in this straightforward sense, not designed. Clouds, for example, are not *for* anything: they are formed by processes of water and air warming and cooling, evaporating and precipitating. We might benefit from the temporary cover of clouds on a hot summer's day, but that's no reason to think that clouds exist for our benefit. Nor do mountains fulfill any function, despite our proclivity for skiing or marmots' tendency to burrow at high altitudes. The French Alps do not exist for either of us: they are the result of the collision of the African and European tectonic plates, along with millions of years of glacial activity and erosion.

Even knowing something about geological processes, some things in nature are so remarkable that it is difficult to shake off the feeling that they *were* designed. About 50 miles north of Dunedin, where I went to university, there is a sleepy little fishing village—population 120—home to maybe my favorite restaurant in the whole world, *Fleur's Place*. The village gives its name to a set of boulders littered across the nearby Koekohe Beach. The Moeraki boulders are large spheres—about 50 of them can be seen now—some up to seven feet in diameter. They are an uncanny sight, like marbles left untidied by naughty giants or an elaborate work of public sculpture. They aren't either of these, of course: they began 60 million years ago as shells and bones and things on the seabed, around which crystals formed, mixed with silt and clay and time.

Despite their remarkable sphericity, the Moeraki boulders were not designed, and neither are natural pearls, though both have since been turned into art and jewelry. There are any number of necklaces and brooches featuring these drops of polished iridescence: and the vast majority of pearls are now cultivated in farms, which produce more than a thousand tons each year. There is a six-foot-tall seven-ton Moeraki boulder mounted at the entrance of the Otago Museum in Dunedin, just next to the university library where I first discovered Deb's work. Images of the boulders appear all over the place, in tourism brochures and on social media accounts the world over. In the cases of both pearls and the boulders, we have imposed our designs on them.

We infer design too, when confronted by such marvels: or at least I do, and I am certainly not alone in this. I have no sympathies with Young Earth Creationists, who believe that the world was created in six days. Nor do I put any stock in much-discussed *teleological arguments* (from the Greek *telos*, "goal") for the existence of God, which begin with observations that some

things in the natural world—biological mechanisms, fundamental physical forces, and the like—are very intricately arranged and conclude that
they must have been designed that way, probably by God. But I fully em-
pathize with the gut feelings behind these sorts of arguments. Some things
in the natural world do seem to bear the marks of a brilliant artist, inventor,
or engineer, even though I believe that there are probably very good scientific explanations for many of nature's miracles, whether it's the breathtaking
beauty of the *aurora borealis*, or the superlative toughness of microscopic
tardigrades, or the nuclear fusion in stars that produces, well, pretty much
everything including the atoms that make up our bodies.

The theory of evolution by natural selection has, since the publication of
Charles Darwin's *On the Origin of Species*, been among the most fruitful and
powerful sources of scientific explanations. It has helped us to understand
how animals came to be able to see, tracing back the evolution of eyes from
rudimentary patches of light-sensitive cells at least as far back as 540 million
years ago.[3] Similarly, it has helped us to understand how animals came to be
able to fly. Flight seems to have evolved independently at least four times—in
insects, pterosaurs, birds, and bats—from limbs in some cases and gills in
others.[4] It is not just the origins of body parts and their functions that the
theory of evolution sheds light on. Most excitingly for psychologists, the
theory also gives us clues about why animals—including humans—behave
the way we do.

My favorite example of this comes from the mating habits of bees, and
other members of the order *Hymenoptera* that includes wasps, ants, and
sawflies. As you may know, bees work to help their mother—the queen—
reproduce rather than heading off to reproduce themselves. At first glance,
this seems to make no evolutionary sense. The modern theory of evolution
tells us that organisms have an imperative to propagate their genes, after all.
But it turns out that bee genetics are not the same as ours. Geneticists have
discovered that bees share 75% of their genes with their sisters but only 50%
of their genes with their children.[5] This means that they actually pass on
more of their genes by helping their mother produce more sisters for them
than by producing offspring themselves!

Despite their obvious opposition, proponents of the theory of evolution
share something in common with creationists and other believers in so-
called intelligent design: evolutionary biologists also use the *language* of design, even in the absence of a designer. They—and we—cannot seem to help
but to talk about the *functions* of biological features, as *designed* by natural

selection or as evolutionarily selected *for* something. Eyes are for seeing, for example. Wings are for flying. There is even a sense in which this is why they exist, but this sense is very limited indeed. Eyes exist because, many many generations ago, organisms that possessed patches of light-sensitive cells reproduced more successfully than their totally light-insensitive peers, thus passing down this trait. Over successive generations, organisms with more or better versions of such cells also outperformed those with worse or fewer, and so it goes until we get the sophisticated if flawed visual organs we enjoy today (and rectify with glasses, which actually are examples of intelligent design).

Eyes exist in part *because* they have given those who had them a competitive edge for generations. However, the processes involved in their evolution—the random mutations that resulted in genes that encode the PAX6 and Rh proteins, the mechanisms of gamete production, the transmission of light from the Sun to the Earth—have no goals, and certainly not to turn a patch of cells into a visual system that permits us to perceive depth and color. There is no literal sense in which evolution *intends* to make eyes, or wings, or anything else. The process is much more like the concretions of the Moeraki boulders than it would seem. Our use of functional language is therefore metaphorical, but it is telling, especially in the hands of an imaginative prose stylist like the biologist-cum-celebrity-atheist Richard Dawkins who writes about the "Blind Watchmaker"[6] of evolution, not unlike the "invisible hand" of free market economics. Even when we know that we live in a "universe without design" as Dawkins asserts, we cannot seem to live without the language of design.

The teleological bias

That's what Deb's paper is about: this feeling, difficult to shake, that things exist for some reason, some *purpose*, which suggests intentional design. "Intuitive theists" is surely an exaggeration, but it is an understandable one, perhaps especially in the US context, where religion has long been associated with the rejection of scientific theories about the origins of the universe and of human beings. One way of thinking about Deb's research is as an investigation into the psychology of people who reject scientific theories, instead subscribing to things like Young Earth Creationism, Intelligent Design Theory, and other such peculiarities of American religion. But this is not how she approached it: indeed, to this day, she does not think of herself as a psychologist *of religion*.

Deb insists that she is primarily interested in how children understand the *natural* world, and especially the biological world, though she recognizes that her work provides insights into religion. Nevertheless, these insights are fascinating byproducts of her core interest, not its central focus. This focus comes across clearly in her doctoral dissertation, completed in 1996 under the supervision of Paul Bloom, a developmental psychologist, now at the University of Toronto. The dissertation opens with a discussion of how common design or *teleological* thinking is among adults, not just among religious people, but also among scientists and philosophers. It then turns to questions about cognitive development, particularly about how children think about the biological world. More specifically, Deb frames her research as a response to the work of the developmental psychologist Frank Keil, who argues that children's teleological intuitions are restricted to humanmade things and parts of living things, like eyes and wings, but not to whole living things or parts of inanimate natural objects, like boulders and pearls. Deb wanted to know if Keil was right, or whether children's teleological intuitions were actually *promiscuous*, applied willy-nilly to all kinds of things: eyes, wings, rocks, pearls, clouds, and the French Alps. This seemingly minor dispute over the scope of a specific quirk of human psychology was the point of her thesis, the theoretical motivation for her experiments, which are now critical for theorists in the psychology of religion.

Puppets in the lab

Psychological research with children is hard. Children—especially the four- to six-year-olds that psychologists like Deb seem fond of studying—are easily bored and often misunderstand our questions. Or, put another way, adult experimental psychologists are very boring and not very good at asking questions. Deb tells me there is no good instruction manual for how to design experiments for children, and that it is a difficult skill to teach. One learns by experience, almost by channeling the children themselves. It is all about attention and comprehension. What questions can children understand? What will they sit through? How do you get them not to run around the place? This is why psychology experiments with children typically require setups with quite high production value compared to those with adults. There is no instruction manual, but there is *lab lore*: and lab lore says that puppets work.

The participants in Deb's first study included 16 children from local daycare centers in Tucson, ages four and five, as well as 16 University of Arizona undergraduates, who served as an adult comparison group. Participants were first introduced to a puppet that was dressed like a king, creatively named King Puppet. King Puppet, they were told, is not very smart: there's a lot he doesn't know, so he asks a lot of questions and sometimes he asks silly questions. There are, contrary to the encouragements of kindly schoolteachers, such things as dumb questions. The participants' job was to answer his questions when they were sensible, and to tell him when his questions were not sensible.

To make sure that the participants understood the task, they had a few trial runs: trial runs are crucial in experiments with children. In these, King Puppet might examined a picture, say of a dog, and ask "Where do you switch the dog off?" This, of course, is a silly question. Most of the participants seemed to get this, certainly after a few of these practice rounds. Then King Puppet would ask a more sensible question, like "Where does the dog like to play?" Now most of the participants could give a meaningful answer, even if the answer was "I don't know." Deb and her team made sure that the participants knew that "I don't know" was a legitimate response: this is important because when children feel as though they cannot plead ignorance, they tend to make nonsense up. Actually, maybe children and adults are not that dissimilar on this point.

All this is preamble for the experiment proper. The experiment took place over two short sessions rather than one long one, to keep the children engaged. In each, the puppet would ask questions about a bunch of different things: familiar and unfamiliar things, humans and animals, humanmade objects like clocks and statues, nonbiological natural objects like clouds and mountains. For each thing, King Puppet would ask what it was for: What's the tiger for? What are the baby's toes for? What's the clock for? What's the jeans pocket for? What's the cloud for? What's the mountain's peak for? As with the trial runs, children would either tell King Puppet that he had asked a silly question, or they would answer the question, even if their answer was "I don't know."

The sessions were all taped, so Deb and her team could return to them later to *code* or categorize them. In this case, the responses were either coded as "functional" when the participants provided answers like "The clock is for telling time" or not, such as when they said that King Puppet was asking a silly question (coded as "silly") or that they didn't know the answer (coded as "other"). To work this out, two people independently read through a transcription of the tapes and assigned each of the participants' answers to one of the three categories. Then Deb checked how much they agreed. Fortunately, they agreed 85% of the time, which is pretty good as these things go. There's always an element of subjectivity with coding, and some disagreement between coders is normal. A third person was brought in to adjudicate on the disagreements.

If Frank Keil was right, children's functional explanations would—like adults'—be limited to humanmade objects and their parts, and parts of animals like teeth and toes. If not, the children would be more laissez-faire about their functional ascriptions than adults are, saying that mountain peaks were *for* a purpose.

The results of this first study fell somewhere in between the two extremes. The children were quite happy to ascribe functions to entire animals as well as nonbiological natural objects and their parts but did not always do so: they gave functional explanations 60% of the time for these, compared to about 80% of the time when it came to biological parts and humanmade objects. They said that tigers were for "see[ing] at the zoo," for example, and clouds were for making rain. Adults were less teleologically promiscuous, but even they thought that whole animals and natural objects and their parts served some function 30%–40% of the time: they drew the line at *parts* of natural objects though, like the peaks of mountains and parts of clouds.

Deb's doctoral dissertation contained several more studies, each refining and building on this first one in different ways.[7] Her second study—featuring actors disagreeing about what things are made for rather than an ignorant puppet—tried to rule out the possibility that what the children meant is just that raining is what clouds *typically do* rather than what they are for or why they exist. Perhaps the distinction between the two is lost on children. (Spoiler: It isn't.) The third and fourth studies—dispensing with puppets and actors altogether—considered whether children also considered *users'* intentions and *accidental* effects when determining what something was for, not only the original designers' intentions. (Not consistently, but more than adults did.) But it was her next set of experiments, which she called her *Pointy Rocks* studies, that piqued my interest most as a graduate student, preparing to design and run my own study.

By this time, I had already decided to work on religion, and her work was gaining some prominence in the field. Recalling that first time I had encountered the paper, I dug it up, bemused that my initial reaction—that finding Deb's paper that first day was a sort of sign—was itself a great example of teleological thinking.

The pointy rocks experiments

Deb ran these studies during her postdoctoral year at the University of California in Berkeley. They are still among her favorite studies, even 20 years later, and mine as well. Having spent her doctoral years studying preschoolers, she took it a little easier this time around: children aged seven to 10 years, who did not need the fancy rigs that younger children's limited attention spans demanded. She did, however, commission a set of drawings for the study, fulfilled by talented undergraduate research assistants. There were four pairs of drawings, each depicting an unfamiliar (but quite real) prehistoric animal and a nonliving natural object. It is entirely possible that my love for these experiments is due to the fact that they feature prehistoric animals.

One drawing was of *Cryptoclidus*, a plesiosaur from the Middle to Late Jurassic period that ended about 145 million years ago: it is one of those long-necked marine reptiles with flippers that people often mistakenly refer to as dinosaurs, not that I am ever tempted to correct them. This was paired with that of the pointy rock that gives the study its name. Then, there was the drawing of *Mononykus*, which Deb called a "terrestrial bird" in the paper, but it *is* a dinosaur: a theropod from the Late Cretaceous, which was admittedly very bird-like. *Mononykus* was paired with a sand dune. *Moeritherium* was paired with a green stone. Deb describes it as a small and squat mammal, but we should imagine something the size of a tapir or a large pig, rather than of a hamster. Finally, there was a "large terrestrial mammal" paired with a pond, which Deb dubbed "Macreuchenia." This seems to be a misspelling of *Macrauchenia*, whose name means "long llama." They only disappeared 10 or 20 thousand years ago, weighed about a ton, and stood over two meters tall without stretching their llama-like necks.

As before, Deb wanted to know whether children see different kinds of things as designed, as having some purpose or function. She had unanswered questions from her doctoral research, as well as ideas about how to improve on those previous experiments. She wanted to know, for example, what would happen if she made children *choose* between different kinds of explanations for why the rock is pointy or why *Cryptoclidus* has a long neck. Confronted with a *non*teleological explanation—the rock is pointy because little bits of stuff piled on top of one another over time, and so forth—would children still prefer a teleological one? Deb also wanted to know if children preferred some kinds of teleological explanations over others. For example, the rock might be pointy to protect itself from marine reptiles; or it could be pointy to serve as back-scratching device for those reptiles. The rock's pointiness might be to benefit itself or to benefit others. Deb also wanted to know how children's thought about these things changed as they got older and learned more about scientific explanations.

Both of the Pointy Rock experiments included four groups of 16 people: adults, who were university undergraduates; first graders, who were about seven years old; second graders, about eight years old; and fourth graders, about 10 years old. They each saw all four pairs of animals and nonliving natural objects, and they were all asked a series of *why* questions about them.

Why do you think Cryptoclidus had such long necks?
Why do you think Cryptoclidus' necks swayed from side to side?
Why do you think the rocks were so pointy?

For each question, they were given two possible answers, and were asked to pick the one that made the "most sense" to them. There was always a nonteleological answer as well as a teleological one: sometimes the teleological one referred to benefits to the animal or object itself (e.g., to protect itself), and sometimes it referred to benefits to others (e.g., for other animals to scratch their backs on).

This second experiment was designed to improve on the first, so they were very similar but for a couple of modifications. She was dissatisfied with some of the teleological explanations in the first experiment, especially those that *anthropomorphized* the animals too much, referring to them loving their babies or having fun with their friends. There's nothing wrong with a bit of anthropomorphism most of the time, but if the other-benefiting explanations were also more anthropomorphic than the self-benefiting ones, then any preferences for the other-benefiting explanations might just be because people enjoy anthropomorphism. Psychologists call this a *confounding variable* or simply *confound* for short. Deb wanted to get rid of this confound.

She also worried that the children were not understanding the task as she wanted them to. She didn't just want children to pick the answers they *liked* because it was funnier or something, but to pick the answers they actually thought were the best explanations for why rocks are pointy, why *Cryptoclidus* had a long neck, and so on. So, in the second experiment, she encouraged the participants to "think like a scientist" when answering the questions. To demonstrate what this meant, the children were told how clouds form. They were given a nonteleological explanation about how clouds get made when water warms up and gets carried as bubbles into the sky where they group together as clouds, congregations of tiny little water drops. This, they were told, is how scientists explain rain. Be like a scientist.

You might think that this preamble would severely discourage children from preferring teleological explanations; Deb suspected it might too. But it didn't, neither for children nor for adults, which is a testament to how strong our teleological intuitions are. It's not quite Deb's intention, but I think of the "that's how scientists explain rain . . . think like a scientist" thing as an attempt to *break the finding*. It's a way of testing how robust a phenomenon is, a bit like a stress test in medicine and engineering. When doctors want to know how your heart is doing, they don't just measure your pulse at rest: they make you run on a treadmill to see how your heart holds up when it has to work hard. Scientists do something similar, to see if their findings hold up in diverse conditions. Physicists, for example, have conducted many tests of Einstein's theory of general relativity. Even the first three so-called classical tests were quite diverse, involving observations of the orbit of Mercury, the deflection of light around the Sun, and changes in light wavelengths from distant high-gravity stars. Since then, there have even been tests of general relativity based on observations of two black holes merging. These different tests provide converging evidence for the theory.

Psychologists sometimes call this approach—of looking to see whether the same effects can be found using different experimental protocols—*conceptual replication*, as opposed to the kind of direct replication that we saw in the previous chapter. Sometimes people argue over which is better, but this is a silly argument to have. Direct replications tell us whether the original effect is real, or whether it is a statistical anomaly. Conceptual replications tell us whether the phenomenon underlying the original effect is robust, or whether it is driven by the idiosyncrasies of a single sample or manipulation or measure. In this way, *cross-cultural replications* like the one Will Gervais conducted about the correlation between the cognitive reflection test and religious belief are a species of conceptual replication.

In her doctoral work, Deb had discovered some evidence that children intuitively believe that things in the world—not just human-made things, but also natural things—are designed. Now, she wanted to know whether this holds up in different situations. There is always the possibility that those initials findings were a fluke, perhaps an artifact of those particular children or that particular puppet show or those particular questions. The doctoral dissertation itself included a few conceptual replications, but she was in a new city now, with new opportunities to try other things to see how robust the finding was.

Deb's second Pointy Rocks study—with the scientific explanation of cloud formation—is a conceptual replication of the first; and both studies are conceptual replications of her doctoral research. Taken together, they give us stronger reason to believe that children do have teleological intuitions about natural things, and not just human-made ones. In the Pointy Rocks studies, as in her doctoral research, Deb found that children were much more gung-ho with their teleological explanations than adults were. She also found that the youngest children in the study were the most willing to endorse teleological explanations and did not really mind whether they were self- or other-benefiting, whereas the older children responded a bit more like adults, endorsing fewer teleological explanations for nonliving natural objects and having clearer preferences for self-benefiting functions than other-benefiting functions. Still, even they preferred teleological explanations for nonliving natural objects over 40% of the time, compared to just over 10% among adults.

Breaking the finding

Deb could have stopped there and moved on to study something else: her collection of studies, each one improving on and extending the one before it, already provided a clear and compelling answer to her question about the scope of our teleological bias. Deb was right, and Frank Keil was wrong. But she didn't stop.

After her time in California, Deb brought the Pointy Rocks study to Boston,[8] where she is now professor of Psychological and Brain Sciences at Boston University. Here, she doubled down on the "that's how scientists explain rain" thing and made a few other small modifications that might be expected to break the finding, and still found the same results. She has also exported the experiment to primary schools in West London, to test it out on seven-, eight-, and 10-year-olds there. The United Kingdom and United States are not *super* different, but the United Kingdom is considerably less religious than the United States. Consistent with this observation, British children were a little less keen on teleological explanations of nonliving natural objects and preferred self-benefiting over other-benefiting teleological explanations, but otherwise behaved more-or-less like the Americans.

As an even more stringent test of the idea that these teleological preferences are *intuitive* as opposed to being the products of cultural indoctrination, Deb took the study all the way to China,[9] one of the least religious countries in the world on various different measures. Religion is not banned in China, but it is discouraged, especially among members of the Communist Party. Unlike in the United Kingdom, where there are plenty of schools run by religious organizations, the Chinese constitution forbids the use of religion to "interfere with the education system." If there is any place on Earth to run an experiment with children with minimal religious exposure, it would probably be China. Even the children of sworn atheists in places like the United Kingdom or the United States may have picked up a good deal of supernaturalistic thinking from the surrounding culture since these cultures are so suffused with religion. Supernaturalistic thinking is not completely absent in China—it isn't completely absent anywhere—but there is very little cultural support for the idea that things exist for purposes. And yet, even in Beijing, children—especially the younger children, the six- to eight-year-olds—preferred teleological explanations for natural objects much more than adults, at comparable levels to US and UK children.

There's more. Deb's research on adults—usually college students—has always shown that they are skeptical of teleological explanations for parts of nonliving natural things like peaks of mountains or parts of clouds. This is, she supposed, a product of scientific education, which reserved teleological language for very specific cases like biological evolutionary adaptations. But if there is something *deeply* intuitive about children's teleological preferences, maybe we can still find it in adults if we scratch a bit further under the surface.[10]

The method was essentially a rapid-fire version of her standard task. This time, instead of having pictures of plesiosaurs and pointy rocks, she presented statements on a computer, which participants just had to classify as true or false. The key statements were scientifically unwarranted teleological statements like

The Sun radiates heat because warmth nurtures life.

The Sun does indeed radiate heat that nurtures life, but it does not do so *because* warmth nurtures life. Adults should reject most statements like this as false. But what if they had to make the judgment under time pressure?

This is a bit like the logic behind the Cognitive Reflection Test (CRT) turned on its head: the CRT assumes that people will give the intuitive—and wrong—answer unless they stop and think about it. Deb's question is whether adults would intuitively prefer teleological explanations when we don't allow them to stop and think about things. Now, time pressure might just lead to all kinds of mistakes, not just mistakes in the teleological direction. So there had to be other kinds of statements in this task, including both true and false statements, teleological and nonteleological statements. Only if time pressure led to more mistakes on the unwarranted teleological statements than these others, could Deb conclude that adults also possessed teleological intuitions. And this is indeed what she found. When the task was not speeded, adults rejected the unwarranted teleological statements about 70% of the time: not *very* consistently, but it is not as though these participants were professional scientists. In contrast, when participants were put under time pressure, they only rejected the teleological statements about half the time. They had no trouble with the other statements, with or without time pressure.

At this point in the chapter, you will know better than to assume that Deb stopped there. Her next move was to test *scientists*. If even scientists—who are ostensibly well-trained at rejecting teleological explanations—fall prey to the time pressure in this way, then we have an even stronger case that the teleological bias is deeply intuitive. With this in mind, she took the task to 80 chemists, geoscientists, and physicists from high-ranking universities in the United States, like Boston University, Brown, Columbia, Harvard, MIT, and Yale.[11] As you might expect, the scientists did better than both college students and other local laypeople: they only slipped up 15% of the time when there was no time pressure. But when they were made to do the task quickly, they accepted the unwarranted teleological statements about 30% of the time. Not terrible, but that puts them on par with those college students without time pressure in the previous study, which must be a blow to the egos of these professors and professional scientists.

And finally, Deb brought this task to China,[12] where adults did better than American laypeople but worse than American scientists, which is further evidence that enculturation and training do make a difference to the intuitive teleological bias, and perhaps that scientific education is more effective on this front than religious restriction. I say "finally," but the work did not really stop here. Deb has helped to design other versions of this task to test people's intuitions that the world and features in it were purposefully *made by some being*: the language is deliberately more overt than in the case of whether things are "for" anything. Studies with this sort of task have been run among American atheists and, again, people in China, and the findings have been similar to the ones we have considered here.

More research

After all this work, Deb continues to study the teleological bias, but this is not to say that she hasn't also branched out. Recently, she has been working on how children learn, including how they can be taught scientific ideas like the theory of evolution by natural selection. This is the flipside, in a way, of the work that made her career about children's intuitions about the natural world that don't require very much teaching at all. Branching out is well and good, but there is something commendable about subjecting the same basic idea to more and more tests, using different methods and in different contexts, and learning more about the phenomenon along the way.

It is difficult to overstate how impressive Deb Kelemen's research program is, starting from a puppet show for children in Arizona to over a dozen studies, all variations on a theme, including direct replications, conceptual replications, and cross-cultural replications. None of the studies are *perfect*: the samples tend to be small, some of the teleological and nonteleological explanations are a bit weird, the translations into Chinese are not always very elegant, but Deb knows all this better than most of her critics do.

I don't doubt that she will keep on trying to break the effect, keep trying to scratch underneath psychological surfaces to see how deep our teleological intuitions go and to find out where they come from. She has more questions too: questions that cannot very easily be answered in a laboratory, like whether the children who reject teleological explanations at a young age are also more likely to grow up to become atheists or, better still, scientists. That would take a longitudinal study to answer. I did point out to her that those children in Tucson are now in their mid-20s, so she could try to track them down. Maybe she will.

4

Is God like Superman?

Design: Mixed
Manipulate:
1. Statement type (within-subjects)
- anthropomorphic v. control
2. Agent type (between-subjects)
- God v. Superman v. Mog, etc.
Measure: Recall accuracy

People believe some funny things about God. Take, for example, the *doctrine of divine simplicity*. This is the view that God is not composed of parts. According to the doctrine, not only does God lack parts like arms and legs, eyes and ears, but God also lacks *attributes* of any kind. God lacks things like age, sex, location, power, knowledge, and goodness. Or rather, God lacks attributes if the attributes are distinct from God: to the extent that God has attributes, they are identical with God. Identity being transitive, this also means that all the divine attributes are identical with one another. God's goodness is God's knowledge is God's power, and God also is power, knowledge, and goodness. In other words, the terms "God's goodness," "God's knowledge," and "God's power" all refer to God, as indeed does the word "God."

This is not how we usually think of things. You, for example, are not identical with your attributes, whether physical, psychological, or otherwise: nor are your attributes identical with one another. All the same, over the centuries, Jewish, Christian, and Muslim theologians—like Saadia Gaon, Moses Maimonides, St Augustine, St Thomas Aquinas, al-Fārābi, and ibn Sina—have insisted on the doctrine of divine simplicity. They have argued that it is crucial for other theological beliefs like the belief in God's oneness,[1] God's changelessness, and God's freedom, especially from any kind of dependence. It may be an odd doctrine, a little abstruse, but it also happens to be one still endorsed and taught in the main sects of the Abrahamic religions.[2]

Experimenting with Religion. Jonathan Jong, Oxford University Press. © Oxford University Press 2023.
DOI: 10.1093/oso/9780190875541.003.0004

The implications of the doctrine of divine simplicity are somewhat less arcane. Notice that according to the doctrine, God lacks the attribute of *location*. In this way too, God is very different from you and me. We certainly don't lack the attribute of location: I am currently sitting on a train from London Waterloo to Dorset. My location relative to London and Dorset is constantly changing because the train is moving, but at any given moment in time we can say where I am and it is easier still to specify my location within the train itself by providing my carriage and seat number. Physicists tell me that things are not so simple at the subatomic level. They say that, according to the Copenhagen interpretation of quantum mechanics, when a subatomic particle—say an electron—is in motion, it does not really have a location as we normally understand the word. Instead, its location is sort of *smeared* across space, in a way that makes my head hurt. God is neither like us nor like an electron: God just does not have location, not even in a smeared kind of way. One way of saying this is that God is nowhere; theologians tend to prefer to say that God is *everywhere*, though some want to say that everywhere is in God. These are all attempts to express the same thing, which is a denial that God exists spatially. This in turn entails that God cannot undergo any changes in location. Location simply does not apply to God.

The doctrine of divine simplicity also entails that God does not undergo any changes whatsoever. When we say that something has changed, we mean that some aspect or part of them has changed: some physical feature, perhaps, or some psychological trait. But if God does not have parts, then God cannot change. I suppose God could change altogether, but when something is entirely changed, "change" seems too mild a word to describe the transformation.

Furthermore, not having parts means that God cannot really be said to see or hear, to the extent that seeing and hearing are what we do through our eyes and ears, which are parts of us. Maybe we want to say instead that God *detects* things, which is a vague enough word not to commit us to any particular sensory organ. But detection also normally involves some device—organic or electronic or whatever—picking up some signal, like smoke or light or sound. Detection also usually happens in time and space. God, having no parts and not being in neither time nor space, possesses no such devices and cannot literally be said to detect anything. Theologians of all three Abrahamic religions have generally preferred to say that God *knows* things without having to perceive them.

This is all quite standard and orthodox Jewish, Christian, and Muslim theology. Indeed, anyone who *doesn't* believe these things about God would be considered heretical by Jewish, Christian, and Muslim authorities: or, less inflammatorily, they might be said to be *theologically incorrect*.[3] Fortunately for them, most Jews, Christians, and Muslims probably do hold these beliefs, even if they could not articulate the doctrine of divine simplicity itself. At the very least, if asked directly, they would say that God knows everything and is everywhere at all times. Or they would, if they were properly catechized.

The tragedy of the theologian

It is quite possible that you have not encountered the doctrine of divine simplicity very much, even if you consider yourself a practicing Jew, Christian, and Muslim. This is probably because you were *not* properly catechized, which is not really your fault. But even if you have enjoyed a rather good theological education, you might catch yourself and others speaking and acting in ways that are not quite consistent with the doctrine. It says that God consists of no parts, and yet the scriptures of all three Abrahamic traditions speak frequently of God's eyes and hands. In the Hebrew Bible, for example, we are told that Moses was given "two stone tablets written with the finger of God."[4] The doctrine also entails that God has no location, and yet Christians regularly pray, "Our Father, who art *in heaven*,"[5] which certainly sounds like God has a location, namely heaven. The obvious thing to say about this is that the scriptures are using *metaphorical* language. Talk of God's eyes is a poetic way of referring to God's knowledge, perhaps; and talk of God's hands refers to God's power, which, recall, is identical with God's knowledge.

The trouble with metaphorical language is that it is not always easy to spot, especially in texts composed centuries ago in cultures very different from our own. It is easy for us to hear "Juliet is the sun," and understand that Romeo is not claiming that she is a burning ball of hydrogen and helium 333,000 times the mass of the Earth, but what of

> God said, Let there be light: and there was light. And God saw the light, that it was good: and God divided the light from the darkness. And God called the light Day, and the darkness he called Night. And the evening and the morning were the first day.

On the basis of a literal reading of the first chapter of the biblical book of Genesis from which this text comes, many people believe that God made the world in six days. This, despite the fact that God cannot be said to literally *say* or *see* anything, not having vocal cords or eyeballs, as the doctrine of divine simplicity asserts; not to mention the fact that the Sun and Moon seem only to appear on the fourth day, which raises the obvious question of what a *morning, evening*, and even *day* could mean on the first three days.

On the other end of the theological spectrum, some people end up believing *all* religious language—and not just select passages in Genesis—is metaphorical. On this view, all the narrative prose of the scriptures serves as pious fictions for the purpose of transmitting moral norms or encouraging feelings of belonging. Even belief in God becomes just an expression of such values. This kind of functional atheism is no more theologically correct within mainstream Judaism, Christianity, and Islam than the rampant anthropomorphism of literalists who would have God be an invisible powerful humanoid, a bit like Superman and an all-knowing computer rolled into one, but better.

All of this is to observe that we have inconsistent pictures of God in our heads: the theologically correct ideas as well as the florid metaphors that appear in our scriptures and songs and common conversations about God. Religious authorities would probably like the theologically correct views to hold greater sway in our minds, but this seems quite unlikely. The cognitive anthropologist Pascal Boyer calls this the *tragedy of the theologian*.[6] The cognitive odds are stacked against orthodoxy, not only in the Abrahamic faiths but also in other religious traditions that have subjected their doctrines to philosophical scrutiny. Theravada Buddhism, for example, is a famously *atheistic* religion. Indeed, scholars of religion who debate furiously over how to define "religion" often cite Theravada Buddhism as a counterexample against definitions that revolve around belief in gods. And yet, anthropologists consistently find Theravada *Buddhists* speaking and behaving in their rituals as if the Buddha were a deity[7] in much the same way that Christians often speak and behave—and paint—as if God were an old, usually bearded, man in the sky.

On cognitive schemata

It doesn't really take a social scientist to notice that religious people hold multiple mutually inconsistent views about God: most religious people themselves would, on some reflection, recognize it too. Certainly, it was not lost on Justin Barrett, growing up in a Christian family and attending Calvin College, a university named for the Protestant Reformer who once wrote that the human mind is a *factory of idols*.[8] The doctrines he was formally taught were palpably different from the images of God that featured prominently in the songs he sang at church. By the time he left Calvin for graduate school at Cornell, he knew that he wanted to study how these different *god concepts* worked: he wanted to inspect the factory of idols in a psychology laboratory.

At Cornell, Justin joined Frank Keil's lab, whom we have already met in the previous chapter: his work on children's biological reasoning inspired Deb Kelemen. In fact, Deb and Justin were formulating their ideas around the same time. While Deb was designing her experiments on teleological thinking, Justin was trying to figure out how to study people's god concepts. One day, while discussing research with other graduate students and researchers at Cornell, someone reminded Justin of John Bransford's work on memory in the 1970s.

In the old days, even until the 1920s, most people who thought about this kind of thing assumed that memory worked a bit like an attic: it was a store for things—memories—to be kept until they were needed again. Sometimes we are unable to find what we are looking for, and this may be because it's hidden among some old clothes or because it's been eaten by moths. Memories, too, can be jumbled up and damaged. But then in 1932, Frederic Bartlett—the first-ever professor of experimental psychology at the University of Cambridge—published his book *Remembering*, in which he describes a new theory that memory is a reconstructive process.[9] Rather than being like an attic full of stuff, memory is more like a bin full of Lego bricks: whenever we recall an event or some information we are rebuilding an approximate copy of what we experienced before. Bartlett's theory also posited *schemata*, which are tacit instructions—a bit like blueprints or scripts—that tell us what to do, including what to pay attention to and how to rebuild memories.

Psychologists' favorite example of a schema is that of going to a restaurant. Once we know that we are in a restaurant—as opposed to being at home or being at the ballet—we immediately have a set of expectations that guide our behavior. When a nicely dressed man comes and asks if we would like something to drink, we are not surprised and do not tell him to mind his own business: we know that restaurants employ waiters whose job it is to ask such questions. We know also that we will eventually have to pay, which we probably would not have to at home. These expectations are all parts of our schema for dining at a restaurant.

More generally, schemata help us understand things, which is where John Bransford's work comes in. Consider the following passage from his 1972 paper with Marcia Johnson:[10]

> The procedure is actually quite simple. First you arrange things into different groups depending on their makeup. Of course, one pile may be sufficient depending on how much there is to do. If you have to go somewhere else due to lack of facilities that is the next step, otherwise you are pretty well set. It is important not to overdo any particular endeavor. That is, it is better to do too few things at once than too many. In the short run this may not seem important, but complications from doing too many can easily arise. A mistake can be expensive as well. The manipulation of the appropriate mechanisms should be self-explanatory, and we need not dwell on it here. At first the whole procedure will seem complicated. Soon, however, it will become just another facet of life. It is difficult to foresee any end to the necessity for this task in the immediate future, but then one never can tell.

Most people find this bit of text baffling. And when asked to recall what they have read they cannot do so very well. You might be able to relate. Now, if before you read the passage, I told you that it was going to be about *washing clothes*, the whole thing might have made much more sense: having understood it better, you might also be able to remember it better. This is what Bransford and Johnson found in their experiment. The theory is that being told what the passage is about activates our schema for doing laundry. This in turn helps us to remember the passage because we actually already know a lot about its contents: when we recall the passage, we can rely on our schema as well as on our recollection of the actual words we read. We can use our schematic knowledge to fill in the gaps in our memory.

In a later study, Johnson, Bransford, and Susan Solomon looked more closely at this gap-filling role that schemata play.[11] They had participants listen to a series of short stories like:

> John was trying to fix the bird house. He was pounding the nail when his father came out to watch him and to help him do the work.

Notice that the story does not mention a hammer. You might well infer that John used a hammer to pound the nail, but he could have been using his shoe or something else instead. The participants were then shown a series of sentences, and they had to decide whether or not each sentence was from a story they had just heard. For example, the sentence "He was pounding the nail with a hammer" was *not* in the story, but participants often misremembered hearing sentences like this, probably because their schema for how people use nails involves hammers.

Uncovering religious schemata

Justin figured that this classic research about memory could be applied to tell us something about people's tacit assumptions—their schemata—about God. He could tell people stories, and see how people *mis*remembered them, see what theological hammers would slip into their memories. He began to construct stories like the story about John fixing the bird house, but about God answering prayers, comforting people, rewarding good behavior, surveying creation, and so forth. It was hard work, and hard to get right. The main challenge was that of leaving genuine inferential gaps without *leading* participants to fill them in a particular way. An example might help to illustrate what I mean:

> A boy was swimming alone in a swift and rocky river. The boy got his left leg caught between two large, gray rocks and couldn't get out. Branches of trees kept bumping into him as they hurried past. He thought he was going to drown and so he began to struggle and pray. Though God was answering another prayer in another part of the world when the boy started praying, before long God responded by pushing one of the rocks so the boy could get his leg out. The boy struggled to the river bank and fell over exhausted.

Notice that the story does not tell us that God stopped or finished answering the other prayer before pushing the rock. However, it does use temporal language—"before long"—and this might encourage readers to assume that God did stop answering the prayer to help the boy. Talk of God "pushing" might also encourage participants to think anthropomorphically. The word "moving" may have been better. Critics of Justin's work still point out the pitfalls of these nuances of language, but he is well aware of these issues too.

If the stories are flawed, it was not for lack of trying. The process of writing and revising these stories was arduous, and he did not do it alone. He work-shopped the stories with graduate students and collaborators to try to weed out these little problems. He also wrote up eight of these stories, rather than relying on just one: this makes it less likely that whatever effects he finds are just artifacts of the way each story is written. And—like Deb Kelemen—Justin also ran several versions of this study to make sure that he wasn't simply tricking people into misremembering things but actually discovering something about how people think about God. The paper in which these experiments appear is not uncontroversial, but it is a classic in the study of religious cognition.[12]

The story about the boy saved from the rocks is, for the purposes of the experiment, one about whether or not God is bound by space and time. The other seven stories focus on different traits, like God's ability to see, hear, and smell. As we have seen, the theologically correct answer for Jews, Christians, and Muslims to the question about God's relationship to space and time is that God is not bound by them: God can answer any number of prayers simul-taneously regardless of where the petitioners are located. Similarly, adherents of the Abrahamic religion should believe that God's way of knowing does not require the senses of vision, audition, and olfaction. However, this does not necessarily stop God from knowing what something looks, sounds, or smells like. Crucially, God's ability to know what things look, sound, or smell like cannot be thwarted, occluded by a cloud of dust, drowned by the din of jet engines, or overwhelmed by sewer stench.[13]

This first study in the paper is a mirror of John Bransford and Marcia Johnson's Hammer experiment. For each of the eight stories, participants first listened to the story, and were then asked a series of innocuous questions about it.

> Who do you think was the main character?
> Do you think the author was male or female?
> Do you think they were younger or older than thirty?

These questions provided a delay between listening to the story and the sub-sequent recognition task. Unlike in the Hammer experiment, participants were not asked to recognize exact sentences from the passage: instead, they listened to plot points, and were asked whether or not that information was actually in the story.

Some of the statements—like "The boy was swimming alone" and "God responded to the boy's prayer by pushing a rock"—were in the story: others— like "The rocks were moss-covered" were errors. These items would allow Justin to look at participants' baseline accuracy levels. The items he really cared about, however, were the ones that implied anthropomorphic limitations for God, like "God had just finished answering another prayer when God helped the boy" or (my personal favorite) "God stopped helping an angel work on a crossword puzzle to help the woman." These do not actually appear in the stories, but they are perfectly reasonable inferences if we assumed that God was subject to temporal and spatial limitations.

Participants were generally quite good at picking out true and false statements about the passages: the average baseline accuracy was above 85%. In contrast, they were really quite bad with the anthropomorphic items, getting less than 40% of those right. Even correcting for baseline accuracy, they only got 45% of the anthropomorphic items right: they would have done better if they had just flipped a coin. Justin took this as tentative evidence that people came to the task with *tacitly* anthropomorphic assumptions about God. But just because Jewish, Christian, and Muslim theological authorities would consider such anthropomorphism heretical this does not mean that Justin's participants—22 religiously diverse North American undergraduates—would accept the orthodoxy. To check that they did, Justin asked some of the participants overtly about their God concepts. Nearly all of them agreed that God could read minds, was omniscient, could multitask, and could detect things without being nearby. People were less sure about how to express God's relationship to space, but none of them thought that God could only be at one place at a time or that room needed to be made for God for God to be anywhere. There was therefore a stark difference between what people *said* they believed about God and the schemata of God that they brought to reading, comprehending, and remembering stories about God.

This little check was very informative, but it also landed Justin into a little bit of trouble. It seems that simply asking participants these questions affected how they performed on the recall task. Perhaps this should not have been surprising: after all, Bransford and Johnson's study taught us that just telling people that they are reading about laundry before they encounter an otherwise incomprehensible passage changes the experience and facilitates memorization. Justin did think to vary the *order* of tasks, so that some people answered the theological questions before reading the short stories, whereas others did things the other way around. This is what allowed him to find out that affirming theological correct statements beforehand affected how people remembered the stories. As soon as he saw this, he fixed the problem, stopped asking the theological questions beforehand, and recruited more participants to compensate for the compromised cases.

This little error also raised an opportunity for a variation of the experiment. Justin turned this accidental discovery into an experimental manipulation. He recruited 15 additional participants and always had them affirm their theological commitments beforehand. Much as during the earlier check for theological correctness, these participants were asked:

- whether they thought that God could be in multiple places at once
- whether God could do multiple things at once
- whether God needs senses to gather information
- whether God can accurately sense multiple things simultaneously
- why they held the beliefs they did

Again, most of the participants reported fairly orthodox views, though they varied in how well thought through the responses were. They did do a little better than the participants who did not affirm theologically correct views: on average, they rejected the anthropomorphic information 47% of the time. It is somewhat surprising that they did so poorly despite just having affirmed theologically correct beliefs. This may be an indication of how powerful people's tacit anthropomorphic assumptions are. This is reminiscent of Deb Kelemen's finding that explaining cloud formation to children beforehand failed to dissuade them from thinking teleologically about pointy rocks. Or it could be an indication that the short stories themselves encourage anthropomorphism: though if this is all that's happening, the theological affirmations should have made no difference at all.

There is another way to see if the recall errors are driven by participants' tacit assumptions about God or by the stories themselves, which is to take God out of the equation altogether. Justin ran a third version of the experiment, using more-or-less the same stories, but replacing "God" with a novel character about which participants had no tacit assumptions. *Uncomp* was a supercomputer, composed of microscopically small disks that cover the entire surface of the earth. The disks enable Uncomp to sense things without directly touching them: Uncomp can see and smell and hear and even read minds by measuring our brains' electrical outputs. The disks also enable Uncomp to move objects and even to manipulate human brains and therefore our thoughts and feelings. Uncomp is such a powerful computer that it can sense any number of things and can perform any number of actions all over the world at any time.

In short, Uncomp has god-like properties without being God. Unlike God, there are no cultural reasons for participants to anthropomorphize Uncomp: there are no Bible stories or hymns that describe Uncomp in human-like ways, no stained-glass windows that depict Uncomp as a bearded king on a heavenly throne. There should therefore be no tacit anthropomorphic assumptions about Uncomp per se: and so, participants should make fewer anthropomorphic recall errors about Uncomp than about God. And they do, but again not by very much. Participants correctly rejected the target items about half the time. Here again, there are two ways to receive this result. On one hand, the fact that participants do better with Uncomp than God with more-or-less the same stories implies that participants' prior beliefs about God affected how they read the passages. On the other hand, the fact that participants also tend to anthropomorphize Uncomp—about which they should have no tacitly anthropomorphic assumptions—indicates either that the stories themselves encourage anthropomorphism or that people are just promiscuous anthropomorphizers or, indeed, both.

Justin was not quite satisfied with these studies either, so he ran a conceptual replication with even more story variations. This time, instead of having participants listen to the stories and sentences, he had them read. This allowed them to take more time to attend more closely to the stories, which might help them avoid recall errors. It's a sort of reversal of Deb Kelemen's experiment with scientists, where they were forced to respond quickly, and made more teleological errors as a result. In Justin's slowed down version of his experiment, one group of participants read the stories featuring God; another group read the same stories, but were asked about their theological beliefs beforehand; yet another group were first explicitly encouraged to think of God as "radically different from a human." These latter two versions would help Justin find out how robust people's tacit assumptions about God were, and whether they could be overridden.

Another two versions of the stories were written in the manner of Uncomp, to see how much difference the main character makes. In one case, God was replaced with Superman. Superman is, of course, a humanoid space alien, about whom people make perfectly appropriate anthropomorphic assumptions. In the other case, Justin invented three "beings from another dimension of existence"—Mog, Beebo, and Swek—who each had some Godlike properties: lack of spatial location, lack of sensory limitation, infinite attention, infinite ability to move objects and change minds, and so forth. To keep things simple, each of the beings only had a small number of the divine attributes, as was relevant to the stories in which they featured. As it was with Uncomp—and quite unlike Superman—participants were not expected to have any tacit assumptions about Mog, Beebo, and Swek, anthropomorphic or otherwise. The beings also had a leg up over Uncomp: unlike Uncomp, they were not designed by humans. Perhaps participants anthropomorphized Uncomp because it was a product of human concerns: not so with Mog, Beebo, and Swek. Justin wanted to know if participants would treat God more like the humanoid alien Superman or more like these extradimensional beings. So, there were five conditions in total, each with 16 participants: I don't know what it is with Deb and Justin and their preference for the number 16. Maybe it's a lucky number in lab lore.

As with the first study, baseline accuracy was generally high. This time, participants did better than before at calling out anthropomorphic intrusions about God: adjusting for baseline accuracy, participants who read the stories about God answered those items correctly around 60% of the time. The most interesting comparison is the one between this basic condition and the one with the extradimensional beings. They were designed to be like God, but participants should not have had any tacit assumptions about them. So, if participants committed fewer errors in this condition, then the errors about God probably come from participants' tacit assumptions about God per se.

In vindication of the short stories against accusations that they force anthropomorphic responses, participants were correct more than 85% of the time—90% when correcting for baseline accuracy—when the main characters were these extradimensional beings. People definitely treated God like Superman more than like these beings: accuracy rates were quite comparable in those two cases. Also, the two attempts to override participants' tacit anthropomorphism of God were not very successful. Neither answering theological questions beforehand nor being encouraged to think of God as radically different from humans helped much.

These results must have been very pleasing to Justin, but it took one more study to really convince him. This one is much simpler in design: he took four of the stories, had participants read them—13 this time, not 16—and then on the very next page, paraphrase what they had just read. The participants' paraphrases were then given to two independent coders who checked the paraphrases for errors, the inclusion of details not in the stories themselves.

Half of the paraphrases contained anthropomorphic intrusions—God could not hear the birds because of the jet engine, that sort of thing—whereas there were almost no errors of any other kind. Justin takes this as evidence for the sheer strength of people's tacit anthropomorphism of God: these theologically incorrect assumptions were not only affecting people's ability to recall stories, but also their *understandings* of the stories.

Reading religion together

Justin wanted to know what people believed about God: but instead of just asking them, he observed how they read and interpreted stories. There is something apt about this method of studying religion. It is, after all, how all successful religious traditions spread their ideas, even when they have more abstract creeds to be memorized and recited regularly. If we want to understand religion, we will certainly need to study the way religious stories are told and transmitted, received and remembered. Humanities scholars do a lot of this work, of course: university departments of theology and religious studies are full of textual experts and folklorists, whose job it is to study texts and oral traditions. Psychologists really ought to work with them more. We should not be ignorant about what religious stories are like in the real world. Justin's vignettes were inspired by stories that he found in Christian scriptures, but they were still products of his own mind, constructed and constrained by his scientific concerns. Perhaps they are very good facsimiles of the ways in which people actually tell and hear stories about gods—he knows evangelical Christianity well, from the inside—but even so, they are at some remove from the real things.

Humanities scholars might benefit from collaborations with psychologists, too. For example, textual scholars are often interested in how a text's original audience would have understood it: psychologists cannot travel through time, any more than we can read minds, but we might be able to help them figure out what the psychologically plausible interpretations are of the text in question. Historians are also interested in how religious traditions spread, and psychologists might be able to say something about what makes some ideas and stories catchier—easier to understand, remember, and transmit—than others.[14] Psychology is certainly no replacement for other methods, but may be a complement to them. That's Justin's goal, anyway, to work together across disciplines, with scholars of diverse kinds. He is convinced that's the only way we will understand something like religion, which moves in the nexus between cognition and culture.

It's an ethos shared by most people in the field—called the *cognitive science of religion*—that Justin helped to establish. Most of the psychologists featured in this book are involved in this field in some way, but Justin was one of its architects in the 1990s. At the time, he was the only psychologist involved: the others—people like Pascal Boyer, Harvey Whitehouse, Thomas Lawson, and Robert McCauley—were anthropologists or philosophers. Historians of religion got to the table pretty early too: these days, there are evolutionary biologists, neuroscientists, computer scientists, and theologians involved too. The cognitive science of religion is aggressively interdisciplinary, and psychologists play a much larger role than before, in no small part thanks to Justin's early work.

He worked on all kinds of things in those early days after his doctoral work. He ran studies on the spreading of supernatural ideas,[15] beliefs about the effectiveness of rituals,[16] and beliefs about prayer.[17] It is quite a contrast from Deb Kelemen's single-minded focus on teleological thinking, though Justin did bring his anthropomorphism experiment to India to replicate the finding among Hindus.[18] It is not that he disagrees with Deb's approach: he expresses great admiration for her work and career. But he had a different role in a nascent field. He wanted to show that we *can* do experimental psychological research in this space. To do so, he felt that he needed to provide multiple proofs of concept, prototypes for how we can proceed. Twenty years later, he has a lot of people convinced: those of us who continue to run experiments on religion are walking in Justin's footsteps, often knowingly so.

The goal that binds together the men and women in this book is to figure out what it is about human beings that makes us religious. And that job often requires us to peel away religion itself—the theologically or, indeed, *a*theologically correct things we have been taught to say—to see what is going on underneath. This is as true of Deb Kelemen's work revealing the teleological biases underneath secularists and scientists as it is of Justin's work revealing the anthropomorphic biases underneath well-catechized Christians. It is true of most of the studies we will consider. This peeling back is tricky work: history and culture form hard shells around us all, as do our individual desires to keep our heresies close to our chests. Even if we were to confess them, it is unlikely to be in a psychology laboratory. Then again, Deb and Justin do seem to have made some cracks to let some light through.

5

Do children believe in souls?

> Design: Within-subjects
> Manipulate: Physical v. mental
> - body parts/objects v. memories
> Measure: Duplicability
> - self-report measure

Consider the ship of Theseus. Having slain the Cretan Minotaur, Theseus voyaged back to Athens and to his father, the king: it proved a tragic journey, as he came to lose both wife and father before its end. All the same, the ship of the triumphant hero was preserved, and as planks decayed with age and weather they were replaced with newer, stronger timber. Over the centuries, fewer and fewer of the original planks remained, until none were left. Writing in the first century CE, the philosopher and biographer Plutarch notes that the ship had become an illustration for philosophers, who wanted to know whether the ship as it stands now is *the same* ship as the one that bore Theseus home.

Or consider the Experience Machine, which would give us any experience we desired: it would stimulate our brains so that we believed and felt that we were writing a great book about experimental psychology or that we were huddled up with our family in front of a cozy fire or that we were on a tasting tour of the world's best restaurants. Crucially, we would be unaware that the experience was illusory, that in reality, we were actually suspended in a tank, our brains wired up to a powerful computer. Would we, asks the philosopher Robert Nozick, choose to live plugged in to the Experience Machine?[1]

Or consider the Trolley Problem.[2] You are the driver of a runaway tram: the sense in which you are its *driver* is therefore minimal. The tram is hurtling down the tracks as trams do, and as it rounds a bend you notice five workmen repairing the tracks totally oblivious to the oncoming vehicle. It is too late for them to leap to safety, and your brakes are not working! You notice that you can manually turn the trolley so that it takes an alternative route. But on this route, there is a single workman on the track ahead. Like the five before, it is

Experimenting with Religion. Jonathan Jong, Oxford University Press. © Oxford University Press 2023.
DOI: 10.1093/oso/9780190875541.003.0005

too late for him to move off and he will surely die if you switch tracks. *Do* you switch tracks, thus killing one to save five? Or do you do nothing, permitting the death of five by your inaction?

If the experiment is the poster child of the scientific method, then the *thought experiment* plays that part in philosophy. Just as experiments focus our powers of observation, thought experiments focus our powers of imagination, and help us to understand our intuitions better. The philosopher Daniel Dennett likes to call them *intuition pumps*, a tool to help us think or at least to figure out what we think. Our response to the ship of Theseus, for example, tells us whether we think that our physical parts make us who we are. If we feel that the ship is no longer the same ship as it was before, then perhaps we are no longer the infants from whom we developed: after all, the atoms present in our bodies at birth have long since been replaced by other atoms through the natural processes of breath, digestion, and the rest. Using the ship as an example allows us to test our intuitions using a less controversial case than our own bodies.

Similarly, the Trolley Problem originated in a paper by the philosopher Phillipa Foot about the ethics of abortion. She begins with the observation that people generally deem it permissible for the tram driver to turn the tram, thus killing one to save five. This scenario is compared to others with the same outcome in terms of lives saved and lost: imagine, for example, that there a five terminally ill patients who can be saved if only you—the biomedical scientist—killed this one other person to make a serum out of his dead body. Do you kill one man to save five? These examples were meant to help us think about the conditions under which we are permitted and forbidden to take one life to save another. Perhaps we may do so when the taking of the life is not directly intended but is a byproduct of some other action. Perhaps we may do so when we owe duties toward the person saved, but not toward the person sacrificed.

The Experience Machine is not itself about ethics but does have ethical import. It comes from a venerable philosophical tradition of asking questions about reality, and how we might come to know anything about it. Could we not as easily just be brains in a vat? How would we be able to tell in any case? These questions might be familiar from the Wachowskis' 1999 classic sci-fi film *The Matrix*, which explores the idea of the Experience Machine writ large to great effect. Nozick's main goal was to figure out whether pleasure is the only good, as some philosophers have argued. If all we are called on to do is maximize pleasure, then a world in which we were all hooked up to the

Experience Machine would be a better one than our actual reality, in which we do not all get to live out our best fantasies. And so, if we would not want to live in that world, it must be because we believe that there are other goods besides pleasure.

The ethical import of the Experience Machine becomes clearer if we extend it a little. Say, for example, that we have two individuals who have chosen to be plugged into the Experience Machine. In one case, the person chooses to live in a simulated world in which they have a fulfilling job and loving relationships, and in which they practice daily acts of kindness: this is how they derive happiness. In contrast, the other person chooses to live in a simulated world in which they spend all their time bullying others and kicking puppies: this is what makes this person happy, as happy as our first person. Note that in both cases no one is actually receiving generosity or abuse: everyone—and every puppy—except the person plugged into the Experience Machine is an illusion generated by the computer. No one but the individual in question gains or is harmed by their imagined actions. So, the overall happiness levels in the two cases are equal and very high. Have both people made *morally* equivalent choices? If we think not, it must be because we think that there is more to morality than the maximization of happiness.

Philosophers are a funny sort, whose company I have the great pleasure of keeping, not least because they supply me with fun thought experiments like these that have influenced the way I think about deep questions concerning the constituents of reality, the means of knowledge, and what it means to live a good life. But it's not just philosophers who use thought experiments: scientists do too.[3] In fact, one of the best-known thought experiments comes from physics. You may be familiar with Schrödinger's cat, much beloved by science popularizers to illustrate the strangeness of the world described by quantum physics. When the Austrian physicist Erwin Schrödinger first devised the thought experiment in 1935, he actually intended it to serve as a criticism of the Copenhagen interpretation of quantum mechanics, not just as an illustration of it.

Schrödinger has us imagine a cat in a steel box. Also in the box is a device made up of a Geiger counter, a hammer, a tiny bit of radioactive substance, and a vial of hydrocyanic acid. There is such a tiny amount of radioactive substance that within an hour there is a 50-50 chance that one atom would decay. If and only if a single atom decays, the Geiger counter would pick this up and trigger the hammer to smash the vial, releasing the acid that would immediately turn into a gas and poison the cat. Say now that exactly an hour has passed, and we are confronted with the unopened box: is the cat dead or alive? Schrödinger assumes that we might say we didn't know, and certainly that the cat was *either* dead *or* alive. However, on the Copenhagen interpretation of quantum mechanics the cat would simultaneously be dead and alive, or more accurately it would have "the living and dead cat . . . mixed or smeared out in equal parts."[4] Schrödinger thought that this violation of our intuitions was absurd and unacceptable—and Einstein agreed—and so the Copenhagen interpretation had to be mistaken. Unabated, it remains the most popular view among physicists, and Schrödinger's cat has become its mascot.

Thought experiments and real ones

There are thought experiments in philosophy, there are thought experiments in science: and then, there are thought experiments that begin in the armchairs of philosophers and end up in science laboratories. The most famous case of this is probably the *false-belief task* used to investigate how children learn to reason about other people's minds. In the most popular version of the task, we begin with two characters, Sally and Anne. Sally has a basket, and Anne has a box. Sally also has a marble, which she puts in the basket as Anne looks on. Sally then leaves to go for a walk. While she is out, Anne removes the marble from the basket and hides it in her box. Later on, Sally returns. Where will Sally look for her marble?[5]

The answer is obvious to us, of course: she will look in her basket, where she left it. We know that Anne has moved the marble, but we also know that Sally does not have the benefit of our knowledge on this matter. What researchers have discovered is that not everyone passes this test so easily. For example, children under four-years-old consistently fail, saying that Sally will look in the box: they do not seem to differentiate between what they know and what Sally knows.[6] Children with autism also often fail the test, even well after the age of four.[7] The false-belief task has been a standard tool in the psychologist's experimental toolkit since its first use in 1983, but the idea first appeared in a commentary by the aforementioned philosopher Daniel Dennett to David Premack and Guy Woodruff's 1978 paper "Does the Chimpanzee Have a Theory of Mind?," one of the most influential psychology papers ever published.[8]

Besides this kind of crossover from philosophy to psychology, there is now an entire discipline called *experimental philosophy*, which typically involves seeing how people respond to thought experiments. Traditional philosophers like Philippa Foot and Robert Nozick, who construct thought experiments, often assume that their readers will respond in the same way as themselves, and that there will be great consensus on our intuitions to the scenarios. But whether this is so is an empirical question, and one that occupies many experimental philosophers. There are now dozens of empirical studies on the Trolley Problem, which examine how our moral intuitions vary in subtly different versions of the scenario. The ship of Theseus and the Experience Machine have also been used in research of this kind.[9]

Quiddity, haecceity, and a murderer's cardigan

Bruce Hood is a developmental psychologist, having cut his teeth on *object permanence* research in the 1980s. He ran studies to find out whether five-month-old infants knew that things continued existing even when they disappeared from view. This is *classic* developmental psychology. Consider a bit of knowledge that adults take for granted—objects persist even when they are out of sight, objects fall when they are released above the ground, people cannot see what we are doing when their backs are turned to us—and ask whether children and infants know it too. And if they do, how do they? Is it learned, or is it somehow a part of our genetic inheritance? This sort of thing is bread and butter, like the study of prejudice is in social psychology or Shakespeare in English literature.

It took Bruce a while to get started studying supernatural beliefs, though he says that his earliest interest in psychology was sparked by Uri Geller the Israeli-British illusionist and self-proclaimed psychic whose heyday was in the 1970s. I am told he was the David Copperfield of the time, who was in turn the David Blaine of my youth. After that, I lose touch, but I am convinced on the basis of no empirical evidence whatsoever that every generation has its own great magician. Bruce was convinced that studying psychology would teach him how to be a psychic.[10] I take great comfort from this fact, because my own motivations for wanting to study psychology were also less than scientifically respectable. I thought that it would help me gain pastoral skills before I entered seminary. We were both wrong about the nature of the subject, but I like to think that Bruce was much wider of the mark. In any case, Bruce moved quickly on from wanting to have psychic powers to wanting to know why anyone—including himself and perhaps even Uri Gellar—would believe that such powers were real in the first place.

For the last decade or so, Bruce has worked on a variety of experiments on what he calls *supernatural thinking*, which he defines quite broadly. He includes a lot of what other people would call superstitions, because he thinks that they came from the same places, psychologically. The particular aspect of supernatural thinking that has occupied most of his time is *essentialism*. Some philosophers will be puzzled that Bruce considers essentialism to be a type of supernatural or superstitious belief. The notion that things have essences is still influential among philosophers. The basic idea being that there is something about objects that make them *that* object rather than some other, and that gives them the properties they have.

There is, for example, something that makes water *water* rather than liquid mercury, and which gives water its wateriness: chemists might say that this something—the essence of water—is its molecular structure as H_2O. Philosophers sometimes call this kind of essence *quiddity*, which roughly translates from Latin as "whatness." Similarly, there might be something that makes you *you* in all your unique youness. Some religious people might say that this something is your soul. Philosophers sometimes call this kind of essence *haecceity*, from the Latin for "thisness." As it is with water and you, so it may be that many other things have quiddities and haecceities, from poodles to planets, Singapore to the ship of Theseus. Recall that the point of that thought experiment is about whether it is the planks or something else—something nonphysical—that make *this* ship the same ship on which Theseus sailed and not just its doppelgänger.

Bruce is not really concerned with whether or not there are actually quiddities and haecceities: he is happy to leave the job of sorting that out to the philosophers. What he is curious about is whether and why regular people—not just Duns Scotus, the 13th-century philosopher who coined the term—believe in haecceities, how far this belief goes, and how it shapes other aspects of our thought and action. I would probably have started at the haecceities of human beings, which philosophers discuss as the problem of *personal identity*, but that's not where Bruce began. His first port of call was to think about objects like the ship of Theseus. Or better still, like the late US Senator John McCain's lucky feather, or my wedding ring, or a serial killer's cardigan.

These three objects have nothing whatsoever in common except that we have funny feelings about them. In particular, we feel that they cannot really be replaced, even with an exact replica. McCain would have been very un-impressed if you accidentally tore up his lucky feather and presented him with an identical one: it's just not *his* feather.[11] Similarly, I would feel terrible if I ever lost my wedding ring, and a replacement ring from the same jeweler in Orkney would never feel quite the same. The thing about the serial killer's cardigan comes from something Bruce used to do when he was speaking to a public audience. He would show them a tatty cardigan and ask how many of them would be willing to put it on. He would even offer a prize to those who were willing, just to get more hands raised. And then, he would tell them that the cardigan once belonged to famous English serial killer Fred West, at which point most of raised hands would collapse. The cardigan had not changed physically at all: but knowing that a serial killer had worn it made all the difference.[12]

Around the same time as the shenanigans with Fred West's cardigan, Bruce was also working on his first proper experiment on essentialism, which turns out to be much cuddlier than this business with serial killers might imply.[13] He worked with Paul Bloom, the developmental psychologist whose lab has spawned more fascinating experiments on children than you can shake a stick at. You might recall that he supervised Deb Kelemen's doctoral research at the University of Arizona. A few years after Deb left his lab, Paul wrote an influential book about supernatural thinking in children called *Descartes' Baby*, he of "I think, therefore I am" fame. This made Paul the perfect collaborator for Bruce.

Teddy v. clone

For their first experiment together, Paul, Bruce, and Bruce's graduate student Nathalia Gjersoe recruited 43 children aged between three and six years in the United Kingdom. Mentioning English murderers would have been very age inappropriate. Before the experiment, Bruce and Paul asked parents whether their children had *attachment objects* that they regularly slept with and had had for at least a third of their lives already: about half of the children did and half did not. So, they requested the children who did have attach-ment objects to bring them to the laboratory: these were generally soft toys—such as teddy bears—or blankets. The other children were asked to bring a toy they liked.

The children came one at a time, as is typical of psychology experiments: nobody wants to have 43 children in a laboratory all at the same time unless absolutely necessary. Upon entering the lab and after all the niceties, the child is introduced to a *copying machine*, not to be confused with a copier machine, though perhaps the two are not so different in principle. The copying machine is really just a bit of modified old lab equipment, two identical boxes with dials and cables that open at the front. But the child is led to believe that it can make exact physical copies of whatever you put inside of it. In classic magic show fashion, the child is first shown the boxes open and empty. And then, to demonstrate, the experimenter places a green block into one box but not the other and closes both doors. When the doors reopen, *lo!*, both boxes contain identical green blocks. Uri Gellar would have been proud. A magician never reveals her tricks, but Bruce and Paul do tell us that the second block is just secretly inserted through the back of the box, sight unseen. Developmental psychology often involves lying to children. The children all seemed to understand what was going on, not in the sense that they knew that psychologists were trying to pull a fast one on them, but that they understood that the boxes made exact duplicates of things. Just for good measure, the experimenter repeats the demonstration, this time with toys—a rubber toy followed by a stuffed toy—so that the children can see that the machine works for toys too, not just boring, colored blocks.

Next, the experimenter presents the child with a more interesting proposition. A toy—supplied by the experimenter—is copied, and the experimenter asks the child to choose one of the resulting two objects to take home. The children are now quite happy, having just received a free toy, and so the experimenter cuts to the chase. The child is asked to offer up their own possession to be copied: at this point, four of the children who brought attachment objects flatly refused. For the rest, their toys or blankets get copied just like the green block and the other toys before: of course, because there is in fact no duplicate, the experimenter has to sneakily remove the object from one box to the other before opening that second door. Again, the children are asked which of the two resulting objects they want to take home with them, the original or the alleged duplicate.

The results are as you might predict, especially if you have ever had an attachment object. Mine is a plush toy, *Shamu*, named for the first intentionally captured killer whale, though I did not know this at the time. I have had it since I was three years old and visited Sea World in Orlando, Florida.[14] It has traveled with me all over the world. It has been decades since I have needed it to get me to sleep, but I confess that it still resides by my bed even now, 30 years later. There is no scenario in which I would choose an exact duplicate over the original. In this way, I am like most of the children in Bruce and Paul's study. They were happy to have a copy of the experimenter's toy: about 60% of them chose that one. They were even happy to have a copy of their own toy when it wasn't an attachment object: again, about 60% of them chose that one. There is something intriguing about a—seemingly miraculously—copied object, I suppose. In stark contrast, only about 20% of the children chose a duplicate of their attachment object over the original: frankly, I'm surprised there were that many. Who are these monsters?

This is, admittedly, not the most exciting use for a duplicating machine. Surely, this experiment has told us nothing we did not already know. People make complaints like this all the time about psychological research: that it is all common sense anyway, and therefore that research is a waste of time and money. But a lot of "common sense" turns out to be nonsense. Think of how many pithy proverbs there are that contradict one another. *Birds of a feather flock together*. That feels true. It's just common sense. But also, *opposites attract*, feels true too. Ditto for *absence makes the heart grow fonder* versus *out of sight, out of mind*. And so on. Now, if we ran a study that found, for example, that people who are similar in some obvious way tend to be attracted to one another, we might be accused of having wasted our time because that's just common sense. But this charge would be unfair, as the same accusation would have been cast if we had the exact opposite results! A lot of things that feel like common sense might turn out to be false, and studies like these can tell us whether our deep-seated hunches about the world are right.

This time with hamsters

After a few other studies with the copying machine producing inanimate objects of various kinds, Bruce, Paul, and Nathalia—now a postdoctoral researcher—finally upgrade the technology and begin duplicating hamsters.[15] This was not actually the first time they considered duplicating mammals. Even before they ran the experiment with the attachment objects, they first imagined copying the children's mothers—parents being the ultimate attachment objects—to see how strongly they would prefer the original

Mum over the duplicate. This would not have been very easy to pull off, which is why they ended up working with teddy bears and blankies instead.

The studies with the hamsters answered different questions, not about what the children preferred, but about what they believed about the duplicates. In particular, they wanted to know whether children believed that minds could be duplicated in the ways that bodies can. When I first read their paper, I immediately thought of a storyline in my favorite comic strip, *Calvin and Hobbes*, by Bill Watterson.

In this story, Calvin, our precocious six-year-old protagonist, uses a Duplicator—really, a cardboard box, with the word "Duplicator" scrawled on it—to clone himself, finding that his duplicates looked exactly like him and shared his personality, but not his memories. They did not recognize Calvin's parents, for example, mistaking his mother for a "cruel governess." In other words, while Calvin's physical attributes were duplicated, not all of his mental attributes were.

Bruce's experiments were also about memories, and whether they could be duplicated. The first experiment recruited 23 children as participants, aged five-and-a-half to six-and-a-half. The first thing each child does is draw a picture, on which they sign their name. They are then shown the copying machine, and given the demonstration: green block, soft toy, rubber toy. Just as the children in the previous study, these children also all understood what the machine was doing. Next, the children are shown a real live hamster. Researchers tell them he is special because is born with a blue heart, and that he swallowed a marble earlier that morning and chipped a tooth that was too far back in the mouth to see. This left three physical features hidden from view: a blue heart, a marble in the belly, and a chipped tooth.

Next, the children are invited to show the hamster the picture they'd drawn earlier, to whisper their names into the hamster's ear, and to give it a little tickle, so that the hamster now has three memories. After this adorable little interaction, the hamster is placed into the copying machine, and both doors are closed. A few moments later, the buzzer goes off, and first a single door opens, revealing the original hamster.

The researcher asks if the hamster still has the three physical traits that could not be seen: the marble in his tummy, the blue heart, and the broken tooth. In other words, has the hamster changed physically at all in the machine?

The researcher then asks if the hamster still has the three memories they shared: does he know about your drawing, your name, and that you tickled him?[16] In other words, does the hamster remember the interaction with the child?

Next, the hamster is put away, and the second door opens revealing an identical hamster: the duplicate.

The research asks if *this* hamster has all of the same physical traits and memories as the hamster he had been copied from.

Almost without exception, the children believed that the original hamster remained unchanged: he still had a blue heart and the marble in his tummy and the broken tooth. He still remembered the name, the picture, and the tickling. As for the new hamster, most children—about 80%—believed that it too had a blue heart, a marble in its tummy, and a broken tooth. But when it came to the memories, fewer than *half* thought that the machine copied them over. In other words, most kids thought differently about minds than they did about bodies.

Some of you might share the intuition that memories are not copied over when bodies are, but it is not obvious that you should unless you think that memories are located in a *nonphysical* part of you, your mind. If you think that your body—specifically your brain—and your mind are distinct things, and that your memories live in your mind, which is distinct from your brain, then it makes perfect sense that clones might not possess the memories of the original. But if—regardless of whether you believe that there is such a thing as a mind—you think that memories are stored in the brain, then surely an *exact* physical duplicate of a living thing should also remember everything that original remembers. After all, an exact physical duplicate would include a copy of the original subject's brain.

Though on its face, this experiment isn't really about religion or spirituality, questions about whether our memories are duplicable are just a short step from questions about what human beings are made of: whether we are bodies, or more than bodies. I have just been talking about the "mind" being distinct from the body, but we could easily talk about the "soul" or "spirit" instead, which sounds more religious. Whatever terminology we use, we are discussing what philosophers and theologians call *dualism*. Very roughly speaking, dualists believe that human beings are made of two kinds of stuff: physical stuff and nonphysical stuff. Sometimes, the nonphysical part of us is thought to be necessary for life after death: and so dualism is often associated with religion, though not all dualists are religious in the conventional sense.

It might be reasonable to conclude from this study's results that some children are dualists, at least those who believed that the physical aspect of the hamster could be duplicated but not their memories. But an alternative interpretation bothered Bruce, Nathalia, and Paul. Perhaps those children weren't really dualists: perhaps memories are just odd things, and they didn't think that they were the sorts of things that can be copied in general. Recall that in the Calvin and Hobbes story, *some* of Calvin's mental aspects—his personality—were duplicated, just not his memories. Maybe memories aren't copied over because they aren't really a part of you in the way your heart or indeed your personality are.

This worry led them to re-run the experiment with an additional condition. This time 20 children turned up, who came to the lab twice, a week apart. On one occasion, they saw the hamster being duplicated as in the previous experiment, and on the other occasion it was a *digital camera* that was copied instead. The original camera was also said to contain a marble, accidentally lodged inside; it had a blue battery, and a broken catch. As with the hamster's heart, tooth, and marble, these physical traits could not be seen. Crucially, the researchers also created digital memories with the camera—it was used to photograph the child's drawing; an audio recording was taken of the child saying his or her name, and a video was taken, of nothing in particular, just with the camera on and jiggled about.

They managed to replicate the results of the previous experiment with the hamster: about 80% of the children thought that the physical traits duplicated, but only about half thought that the memories did. But for the camera, the children had no problem believing that both the physical characteristics and the memories were carried over into the new copy: in each case, 85% of the children agreed that duplication had happened. Although a digital camera's memories are not exactly like those of a human being or even a hamster, there is an analogy here: after all, we call the storage device in our cameras a "memory card." So, this finding allowed Bruce's team to be a little more confident that the children weren't just confused about memories in general.

They ran a few more versions of the study, always finding more-or-less the same thing, that children are much more likely to believe that physical traits duplicate than that psychological ones do. In one of them, they found a way to ratchet up children's dualism: they gave the hamster a name, *Dax*. They had 40 children in this study, half of whom went through the original hamster study: an exact replication, and with the same results too. The protocol was exactly the same for the other half, except that the children were told that the hamster was called Dax. Instead of half of the children saying that the psychological traits duplicated, only a quarter did once the original hamster was named. Names are, it turns out, powerful things: they mark us out as individuals, psychologically unique even when physically identical.

Dualism and the afterlife

There are many alleged benefits of thinking of the mind as being distinct from the body. Some people think that it helps us to explain *consciousness*: the basic idea is that there is no way for consciousness to arise out of physical stuff, and so there must be a nonphysical part of us that makes us conscious. Some people think that it makes *free will* possible: the basic idea is that our bodies—being physical objects—ultimately obey ironclad laws of physics that do not provide room for the kind of choices and actions that we experience as free. Again, possessing a nonphysical part may provide the possibility of freedom from the laws of physics or, for that matter, biology and chemistry. But as I briefly alluded to earlier, perhaps the most obvious way in which mind–body dualism is useful is as a way of making sense of how we might survive death. Bodies decay when we die: and if we are just our bodies, perhaps we too just decay into oblivion. If we were *more* than our bodies, however, perhaps that part of us would survive to shuffle off our mortal coils, to move on into the great beyond. And if that nonphysical part of us also carries our memories and our free will and our consciousness, aren't those the essential parts of us?

Whatever their personal feelings about the matter, psychologists are, professionally speaking, concerned neither with the truth or falsity of dualism nor with whether dualism guarantees immortality, consciousness, and freedom. This is not to say that personal feelings don't come into things at all. Scientific ideas and interests don't come from nowhere, and they don't only come from dispassionate readings of philosophical writings about quiddities and haecceities. Even Bruce was first inspired by his awe of a magician. In sober contrast, Jesse Bering was driven by the death of his mother.

Alice Bering had been diagnosed with ovarian cancer long before Jesse went off to graduate school to study chimpanzees in Louisiana with Daniel Povinelli, the famous primate behaviorist. When things took an acute turn for the worse and Jesse returned home to Florida to be with his mother, he transferred back to his alma mater to work with his old teacher, David Bjorklund, a developmental psychologist. Over their final months together, Alice and Jesse talked about difficult things: suffering, death, and the great beyond. Neither of them were particularly religious. She was a secular Jew, and agnostic about the afterlife; he was an atheist and skeptic of all things supernatural. Yet, "Who knows?," she would say to him, "But it's you I'd come back to . . . your brother and sister, they already believe. They wouldn't need any proof. If I can, I'll give you a sign."[17]

She died about a year after Jesse moved home, in the evening of January 19, 2001. The next morning, Jesse was roused by the wind chimes hung on a tree just beneath her bedroom window. "That's her," he caught himself immediately thinking: the promised sign that she was okay. He did not *believe* this in the ordinary sense of the word: it only took a moment—an analytical moment, perhaps, as we considered in the second chapter—for him to override his initial response. But, even if just for a moment, he believed in a sense that Alice was reaching out to him in this most mundane, most innocuous of occurrences. A wind chime, singing in the wind, for goodness' sake.

Jesse's doctoral dissertation is dedicated to his mother's memory: he writes in it that they developed the theoretical basis of the work together through those conversations they had just before her death. I don't know if either of them would want to say that she lives on in this work, but it is certainly true that her memory does. Eventually, Jesse named a character in a series of experiments after her. They are known as the "Princess Alice" studies, but that's another story for another day. Our experiment involves neither a princess nor a hamster, but a baby mouse and an alligator.[18]

The setting is a woodland: there is a pond, a tree, and some bushes and flowers. They are all plastic miniatures on a styrofoam base, and the characters are all finger puppets (puppets again!), but the children are asked to imagine that they are real. They are very good at playing pretend, after all. Enter the baby mouse.

The mouse, the children are told, is strolling in the woods. He loves the smell of the flowers here, and the quiet of the place allows him to think many things. He thinks of his mother, and how much he loves her. He thinks of maths, and how he hopes to get better at it when he is a grownup mouse. He thinks of his sore throat, and how maybe a drink from the pond might be soothing. He thinks of his sore feet, and about how he's not sure how to get back home. And then, just as he is about to have a drink of water, he notices the bushes rustle, and before he can do anything about it, out leaps the alligator, who gobbles him up! The mouse is, the children are told, "not alive anymore." This phrasing was deliberate, to appease parents who were uncomfortable with less euphemistic words like "dead" or "killed."

So, we now have a dead mouse, and as with the duplicated hamster, we can ask children what they think about him.

"Now that Baby Mouse is not alive anymore . . . ," the children are asked:

Will he ever grow up to be a grownup mouse?
Will he ever need to drink water again? And to eat?

In other words, do biological traits survive death? They were also asked about psychological traits.

Does he still feel sleepy? Does he still feel sick?
Can he still smell the flowers?
Does he still love his mother? Is he still scared of the alligator?
Does he still want to go home? Does he still hope to get better at maths?
Does he know he isn't alive anymore?

These are psychological states, to be sure, but they are not all of the same kind. Some are normally closely associated with bodily functions: thirst, for example, and perceptual abilities like sight and smell. These are psychological traits that we commonly understand to be tied to some specific organ like our eyes or noses. Some others are less obviously associated with visible parts of our bodies: desire, knowledge, love. Jesse wanted to know which, if any, of these traits children think survive death.

There were two groups of children in this experiment: 35 preschoolers and kindergarteners, aged between three and six years; and 31 older children, aged between 10 and 12 years. For comparison, Jesse also had 20 adults aged between 18 and 20 years who participated in the study, even though it was obviously designed for children. The adults had no trouble denying that the mouse, now dead, would need to eat or drink again; similarly, they thought that the mouse would no longer feel thirsty or sleepy or sick. They even consistently denied that the mouse could still see, hear, or taste. Upon death, the adults thought, all these traits would cease. But some of the other traits gave them pause. Questions about the mouse's feelings about his mother really stand out: compared to the 0% of adults who thought that the mouse could still be thirsty or hungry, over 60% thought that he still loved his mother. Love, it turns out, is stronger than death.

The children's responses were similar: in fact, they were even more reluctant than adults to deny knowledge, emotions, and desires to the dead mouse. The older children—aged 10 to 12—responded rather like adults did on questions about the mouse being able to grow old, feel thirsty, and see things: but over half of them also thought that the mouse still wanted to go home, and that he knew that he was no longer alive. Eighty percent of them believed that the mouse, now dead, still loved his mother. Almost all the younger children—aged three to six—thought that the mouse still loved his mother: most of them also said that the mouse wanted to go home, and knew that he was no longer alive, and so on. At that young age, not all of them understood that the mouse's biological functions like needing to eat and drink had ceased, but 60% to 70% of them did, so it's not just that they didn't understand that the mouse was now dead. They treated some psychological states—especially love, knowledge, and desire—as especially resilient against mortal decay.

Given Bruce Hood's results with the hamster, it is a pity that Jesse did not ask the children any questions about the dead mouse's memories. Or maybe it is a pity that Bruce did not ask the children in his studies any questions about love, seeing as those experiments came many years later. It would be easy enough to do, putting these two studies together to see if the psychological traits that get duplicated are the same ones that survive death. No one has done it yet, though there have been attempts to replicate Jesse's findings, including in different countries like Spain and Vanuatu.[19] These have not always been *exact* replications à la Bob Calin-Jageman, nor have they found exactly what Jesse's original study did: but the picture they provide is still that children more readily believe that psychological states survive death than do biological and biological-adjacent states.

Bruce's experiments have not yet been directly replicated, though two psychologists at the University of Cologne have run versions of the hamster duplication study on American adults, and found that they too were much more likely to think that physical traits duplicated than that psychological traits did.[20] It seems that many people never grow out of their intuitive dualism, though it is difficult to say how much of this is due to religious indoctrination and other forms of social and cultural encouragement. In some ways, it is less surprising that American adults are intuitive dualists than that British children are.

Suffer little children

The rest of the experiments we will look at are on adults, but we should pause for another moment to consider how important it is to study children. Psychological research on children is hard, and yet the Deb Kelemens, Bruce Hoods, and Jesse Berings of the world believe that it is worth the hassle. Parents are busy and reluctant to sign their children up, drive them to a lab, and sit and wait as experimenters set up puppet shows and ask odd questions, sometimes about pointy rocks, sometimes about death. Children can be uncooperative, easily bored, and distractable. They have limited verbal communication skills, especially when they are younger. Psychologists who study infants and newborns cannot ask questions at all and need to measure other behaviors instead, like where the child is gazing and for how long.

The reason developmental psychologists go to all this trouble is not all that different from the reason Justin Barrett used a memory task and Deb Kelemen used a speeded one. Psychologists are always trying to get underneath our skins. In Justin and Deb's case, they wanted to know how adults would respond when you catch them off-guard. Justin could—and did—ask people about their beliefs about God, but then he received answers that reflected what Christians ought to believe, the "theologically correct" answers. His experiments, however, showed that underneath our orthodox beliefs— or perhaps alongside them—we also harbor anthropomorphic intuitions. Deb asked scientists about their beliefs about causes in the natural world, and she generally received good scientific answers. But her experiments showed that this scientific orthodoxy can also be disrupted under pressure, revealing teleological intuitions. They do not think that Christians are *pretending* to believe in God's timelessness or that scientists are pretending to believe in mechanistic causes. But their studies reveal that these beliefs, earnest though they may be, are hard won, and that the intuitions that preceded them might never really disappear.

To study children is to study human beings at an earlier stage of their indoctrination, whether theological, scientific, or otherwise. With adults, we assume their responses when caught off-guard precede their more considered answers to questions. But a more direct test of this assumption is to find the same intuitions among children who have not yet internalized orthodox answers. Furthermore, studying children allows us to observe the indoctrination—or learning, if you like—as it is happening. Adults do not really ever stop learning and developing, but children are little learning machines, and understanding how they learn might teach us how to teach them better. Deb Kelemen's research has even led her to produce a children's book, *How the Piloses Evolved Skinny Noses*, intended to teach them the theory of evolution by natural selection.

Another thing about studying children is that it encourages us to study other cultures: or it should, anyway. Whenever a behavior or belief appears early in child development, this suggests to psychologists that it may be part of our evolutionary endowment. Its appearance across cultures provides further evidence that these beliefs or behaviors are precultural. Developmental psychological research and cross-cultural psychological research can mutually reinforce one another. Unfortunately, cross-cultural developmental research is rare. Just a few years ago, a team of developmental psychologists reviewed all the studies published in the field's top journals and found that 91% of them were of American, English-speaking, or European samples.[21]

In comparison, psychologists of religion seem to be doing rather well. Deb Kelemen took her experiment to China; Justin Barrett took his to India; Jesse Bering's has been run by others in Vanuatu. However, we could be more thoughtful about our chosen field sites for cross-cultural replication. Deb chose China because it is not a culture that encourages teleological explanations about the natural world: it is quite the opposite of the United States in this way, which is a breeding ground for religious skeptics of evolutionary biology and big bang cosmology. She was trying to break the effect, and China was a good place to do that. In contrast, anthropomorphism is hardly foreign to Hinduism; nor is dualism unfamiliar to the ni-Vanuatu, who traditionally believe that ancestral spirits occasionally visit in the bodies of wild animals. If we really want to know how intuitive anthropomorphism and dualism are, we might need to find cultures that de-emphasize these aspects of religion. Theravada Buddhist cultures might be appropriate. Recall that Theravada Buddhism is technically atheistic; it also teaches *anattā*, roughly the doctrine that there is no soul. Perhaps the children of devout Theravada Buddhists will react differently to Justin's, Bruce's, and Jesse's experiments. Or not, which would be interesting too.

6

What does God know?

Design: Within-subjects
Manipulate: Domain of God's knowledge
- morally relevant v. morally irrelevant
Measure: Reaction time

I know what I know, though I cannot always remember if I know something. But I don't know what you know, and not just because we have never met. I can guess at what you know, but I can't be very confident that I'll be right. I know my wife fairly well, and I would be better at guessing what she knows than what you know, but I still wouldn't get it right all the time. For example, we grew up in different countries—she is from England and I am from Malaysia—and there are bits of popular culture that I assume she has consumed, which she mightn't have. Oddly enough, none of this uncertainly applies to what we know about what God knows. God knows everything. Everyone knows that.

Philosophers who want to get more precise say that:

for every proposition p, if p is true then God knows p[1]

A proposition is just an assertion underneath a sentence. For example, "God knows everything" and "Dieu sait tout" are different sentences by virtue of being in different languages, but they express the same proposition about divine omniscience. The upshot of the philosopher's formula is that if God is omniscient, then any question about what God knows must be answered in the affirmative. We don't even really have to finish reading the question before we can answer in the affirmative.

Does God know that *Paris is the capital of France*?
Does God know that *puppet shows are useful for psychology experiments with children*?

Experimenting with Religion. Jonathan Jong, Oxford University Press. © Oxford University Press 2023.
DOI: 10.1093/oso/9780190875541.003.0006

Does God know that *I am writing in a café-cum-record-store in Oxford*?

Yes, in all cases. The only "Does God know . . . " questions that should give us pause are those that sound like they might be expressing propositions, but are in fact nonsense:

Does God know that *the slithy toves did gyre and gimble in the wabe*?
Does God know that *colorless green ideas sleep furiously*?
Does God know that *friendly milk will countermand my trousers*?[2]

The trouble here is not that these subordinate clauses are *false* but that they are meaningless despite appearing grammatically correct: and this means that they do not actually express propositions. It is not just nonsensical sentences that can be nonpropositional. Take sentences that express preferences, for example. God cannot know that

Strawberry ice cream is gross.
Stephen Fry is funnier than Hugh Laurie.
Ella Mae Lewis is the best wife.

These sentences sound like they express propositions, but they don't really. "Strawberry ice cream is gross" is just a common way of expressing my dislike of strawberry ice cream, and "Stephen Fry is funnier than Hugh Laurie" is a way of expressing a preference for Fry's comedy over Laurie's (albeit a minor one). Similarly, the claim that my wife is the best wife is really an expression of my love for her. So, God can know that I dislike strawberry ice cream, that I prefer Fry over Laurie, and that I love my wife: but God cannot know that strawberry ice cream is gross or that Fry is funnier than Laurie or that my wife is the best, because these are not really things to be known. It is no criticism of God to say that God cannot know these, any more than it is a criticism of God to say that God cannot know whether colorless green ideas sleep furiously.

Things get a bit more controversial when we consider God's knowledge of the future. Some philosophers and theologians say that God cannot know the future because there are no facts about the future yet. For example, "It will rain tomorrow" does not express a proposition, because it is neither true nor false, until tomorrow comes. If there are no facts about the future, then it is no criticism of God that God does not know the future because, again, there is nothing to know. But this does not sit well with most religious people—at least in the Abrahamic traditions—because they tend to believe that God *does* know the future. Philosophers and theologians on this side of the debate argue that divine foreknowledge follows from the idea that God is outside time. Others point out that the trouble with believing that God knows the future is that it seems to undermine human freedom. If God knows, for example, what I am going to eat for breakfast tomorrow, can I still be said to have freely chosen my meal?

Gods: Morally concerned or morally apathetic?

The idea behind Ben Purzycki's experiment bears some resemblance to the idea behind Justin Barrett's. Justin observed that many religious people claim to believe that God is beyond time and space, and that God can know things without seeing or hearing or otherwise sensing. He wanted to know whether people actually applied these theologically correct beliefs when reading and thinking about God. He found that they didn't, really: people's working concept of God was much more *anthropomorphic*, subject to the same limitations as humans and other finite objects. Ben wanted to know if there was something similar going on with people's belief in divine omniscience, not so much in *how* God knows things but in *what* God knows.

God knows everything; and we know God knows everything. But maybe there are some things that we are very confident that God knows, and other things that we are less sure about. Ben thinks about religion in rather practical terms: what would be useful *for us* for God to know? Maybe not "us" as specific individuals, but as communities: what kind of divine knowledge would be beneficial to the group as a whole? God's knowledge of how many hairs there are on my head or how many stars there are in the sky may be impressive, but not very useful except perhaps at pub quizzes or dinner parties. Even practical knowledge like what crops to plant or how to cure an illness is not very useful unless God has a way to give us clear instructions. Alas, the occasional prophet notwithstanding, God does not seem to be a very clear communicator. Across cultures and throughout history, people have tried to hear from their gods with questionable success: divination is an inexact science.

In contrast to these domains of knowledge, God's knowledge of what human beings are up to is obviously useful, if a little insidious. We are all too familiar with the idea of constant surveillance as a means of manipulating behavior, from George Orwell's Big Brother to Jeremy Bentham's Panopticon to Santa Claus, who makes lists and checks them twice. If God cares and knows about our behavior—and metes out reward and punishment accordingly—then we, like children around Christmas, may well be motivated to be morally vigilant. God does not even need to be able to tell anyone anything for this to work: all that matters is that we believe that God knows what we did last summer, or whenever.

This got Ben thinking about how supernatural knowledge and concern about human behavior might be special. It is advantageous for societies to believe that gods care and know about human behavior, and both elements are crucial. If the gods care about our behavior, but do not know what we are up to, their concern is toothless: they have no accurate way of meting out reward and punishment. If the gods know about our behavior, but do not care, they provide no motivation for us to behave according to divinely sanctioned moral norms. This led Ben to hypothesize that people might have a bias toward thinking that God knows about our morally relevant behavior, just as Justin hypothesized that we have an anthropomorphic bias when we think about God's attributes.

The most obvious objection to Ben's hypothesis is that we already know that not all gods care about human affairs in the way that the God of the Abrahamic tradition does. Certainly Jews, Christians, and Muslims agree that God cares about our behavior—certainly those considered moral and religious—and rewards and punishes us accordingly. But this does not seem to be true in other religious traditions. For example, the familiar gods of ancient Greco-Roman religions did not particularly care about human deeds or misdeeds, unless they themselves were the victims of these actions. Nor do the gods of the East Asian religious traditions: Buddhist ethics are very well developed, but deities tend not to feature much in them, except in very particular cases toward specific aims. Rather, the karmic system is, as it were, automated, without the need for divine monitoring. This clear demarcation between morally concerned and morally apathetic gods represents the conventional wisdom, and Ben thought that it was wrong, or at least overstated.

Need for speed

Ben did not train as an experimental psychologist, but he worked out very quickly that we have a thing for reaction times. Cognitive psychologists are obsessed with speed. We have seen something of this already in Deb Kelemen's experiment on scientists. She had them judge statements as true or false to see whether even scientists would recognize teleological statements like "The sun radiates heat because warmth nurtures life" as true. The twist was that when she told them to respond *quickly*, they were more likely to endorse these teleological statements than when they could take their time to deliberate. Deb took this as evidence that scientists harbored teleological intuitions that their scientific training overrides when it can. Less directly, Justin Barrett's switch from verbal to written presentations of his stories was also to manipulate speed: the written form allowed participants to take their time to digest and analyze the information. The Cognitive Reflection Test we encountered in Will Gervais's study also makes the same assumption that quick responses are intuitive responses, against which analytical skills can intervene.

None of these studies *measured* participants reaction times, but there are other psychological tasks that do. As I briefly mentioned in Chapter 1, the basic logic behind the use of reaction times in psychological measurement is that the speed with which we respond indicates something about the strength of associations in our mind. This is not unlike the idea that the speed with which we move is related to muscular strength. According to cognitive psychologists, things like memories, knowledge, beliefs, and even desires are all cognitive associations that can be weak or strong. For example, the knowledge that Paris is the capital of France is a specific kind of mental association between our concepts of "Paris" and "France."

If so, and if reaction times can tell us about the strength of cognitive associations, then reaction times can tell us something about those psychological states. Consider, for example, a test of knowledge: a quiz in which you have to decide whether statements are true or false. Here are two items from this test:

Paris is the capital of France. True.
Beijing is the capital of England. False.

In all likelihood, you would easily have provided the correct responses to these statements. You would have done so very quickly, without hesitation. Now here are another two items:

Canberra is the capital of Australia. True.
Rio de Janeiro is the capital of Brazil. False.

Assuming that you were any good at geography at all, you would have gotten these right too. However—unless you are Australian or Brazilian— you might have taken a smidge longer for these statements than for the first set. You might have had to think a bit to remember. You may even have hesitated in order to remind yourself that Canberra is indeed the capital of Australia, not Sydney or some other large Australian city. Similarly, you may have had to remind yourself that it is Brasilia that is the capital of Brazil, not Rio. These processes all add to the time you would have taken to answer the question.

The ease of a task—and the speed at which we perform it—is not only a matter of expertise but can also be a matter of how strongly we feel about or believe in something. For example, if you offered me some strawberry ice cream, I would *very* quickly decline because strawberry ice cream is gross. If, instead, you offered me some pistachio ice cream, I would very quickly accept because pistachio ice cream is lovely. And if you offered me some chocolate ice cream, I would consider it for a bit and probably accept, because my feelings about chocolate ice cream are positive but mild. When it comes to *beliefs*, we shall turn to an example of a task designed by Adam Cohen, a social psychologist at Arizona State University. Adam's task simply required participants to categorize things—including supernatural things, like God— as "real" or "imaginary."

Car. Real.
George Bush. Real.
Darth Vader. Imaginary.
Moon. Real.
Abraham Lincoln. Real.
Homer Simpson. Imaginary.
God.

As you might expect, believers mostly categorized God—and some other supernatural things—as real, whereas nonbelievers categorized them as imaginary. However, within each group people varied on how quickly they responded, and their reaction times reflected how religious or irreligious they were. The study found that people who reported very high or very low levels of religiosity responded very quickly, whereas more lukewarm believers and nonbelievers responded more slowly.[3]

Ben applied the same idea to measure what people thought about God's knowledge. He even worked with Adam to set the experiment up. Participants would be shown a series of questions

Does God know that Ann gives to the homeless?
Does God know that Jane has stolen a car?
Does God know that Billy helps old ladies?
Does God know that Donald is taking bribes?

to which they answered "yes" or "no" by pressing keys on their keyboard. To see whether people prioritize God's morally relevant knowledge, Ben needed some other questions, which refered to things that God also knew, but which were morally irrelevant. He came up with a set of items that were morally irrelevant while still referring to individual people.

Does God know how fast Joey's heart beats?
Does God know how many teeth Hannah has?
Does God know how many freckles Sharon has?
Does God know how many carrots Barry ate?

This was the crucial comparison: do we respond similarly to God's knowledge about morally relevant and morally irrelevant information about people, or do we respond *faster* to the morally relevant information? On top of these main items, Ben also designed a series of *distractor* items, which served a few different purposes. They added some diversity to the questions so that participants would not get bored. The diversity of items also made it more difficult for participants to guess what the study was about. Psychologists don't like it when participants guess what the study is about in case this awareness affects their behavior. Along the same lines, Ben could also use some of the items to check if participants were taking the task seriously, and reading and responding properly. Less cynically, these items also provide *baseline* speeds, which tell us how quick each participant is in general. Without baseline items, we can't be sure whether we are seeing the effects of belief strength or the strength of participants' *flexor digitorum* muscles crucial for pressing buttons.

Ben also needed to control for other potential variables that could skew his data. Besides finger muscle strength, reaction times can be affected by how quickly we *read*, which is in turn affected by how long or unusual a word is. In the case of single words, differences in word length may be negligible unless we present words like *disestablishmentarianism* or *supercalifragilisticexpialid ocious*. But for sentences, researchers tend to want to keep sentence lengths more-or-less constant. We don't really have hard evidence that this makes a difference, but we take the precautionary measure anyway. Because: lab lore. Ben tried to keep the main sentences at 10 or 11 syllables, the syllabic count being more important than the letter count because he was presenting audio recordings to his participants rather than printed words. The other interesting rule for constructing these sentences was to avoid things that elicit strong emotions: nothing too violent or sexual. Strong emotions mess with reaction times: for this we do have plenty of evidence.[4]

With all of this in mind, Ben designed distractor items that were things that God knows that were not about people:

Does God know the height of Mount Everest?
Does God know how many hairs a lion has?
Does God know the pressure at the Earth's core?
Does God know the distance between two atoms?

Some were puzzling and amusing questions about God:

Does God know how to create a round square?
Does God think in a human language?
Does God ever take time off?
Does God know how many angels fit on the head of a pin?

Some were general knowledge questions for the participants themselves:

Did Mark Twain write Huckleberry Finn?
Does each day have 26 hours?
Does 4 plus 11 equal 15?
Are cumulus clouds made of cotton-candy?

Seventy-four anthropology students at the University of Connecticut participated in the experiment. When asked what they thought about God, 47 of them said that they believed in an all-powerful and all-knowing God. On the face of it, these participants responded in the ways you would expect given their beliefs in divine omniscience: in over 90% of the cases, they said that

God knew about both morally relevant and morally irrelevant things. But the reaction times tell a slightly different story: they were much quicker to respond to the morally relevant questions than to those that were not morally relevant. Responses to morally relevant information took about 650 milliseconds on average, whereas responses to morally irrelevant information took nearly 900 milliseconds: a difference of a quarter of a second may not seem like much, but it is fairly large given the speeds we are working with. Participants were also faster to say that God knows about morally bad actions—*Jen lied to her mother*—than morally good ones like *Ann gives to the homeless*. Maybe anthropology students in Connecticut think of God as more of a punitive figure than a rewarding one.

Aliens v. God

Unlike in the case of Justin Barrett's experiment, there isn't the worry here that people respond more quickly to the morally relevant questions because of the way they've been written. There's no reason to think that they are easier to understand than the morally irrelevant ones: the words and sentence structure of all the questions were quite simple and standardized. However, it is still possible that the bias toward moral information has nothing to do with how people think about *God*: maybe we just respond more quickly to moral information in general, regardless of whose mind the information is meant to be in. To address this possibility, Ben also had to ask participants about some other character, much as Justin did with the beings from another dimension. Besides asking about God, Ben also used aliens, which he called "The Ark."

This was an unfortunate choice of a name, as a psychologist pointed out to him later. Ben had gotten the idea from a Canadian science fiction TV show from the 1970s called *The Starlost* set in a spacecraft called Earthship Ark. However, Earthship Ark—a massive spacecraft built to save people from Earth's destruction—was obviously based on Noah's ark from the Bible, which delivered one family to safety from God's wrath. There is another ark in the Hebrew Bible too, the Ark of the Covenant, featured in the 1981 Harrison Ford vehicle *Indiana Jones and the Raiders of the Lost Ark*: it is the container of the stone tablets on which the Ten Commandments are inscribed, as well as being God's seat for when God meets with priests.[5] Never mind: if anything, the name made it *more* likely that participants would treat these aliens like God, which is not what Ben would have wanted: by choosing a name for the aliens that held religious connotations, he had inadvertently set the bar higher than he could have done. If, despite these religious connotations, participants didn't respond to the Ark as they did with God, that would count in favor of Ben's hypothesis.

The year is 3025. The Ark are aliens who have been observing humanity for the past century. They are superintelligent, psychic, and omniscient: they are aware of everything that happens on Earth. So far, so much like God. The Ark differ from God in that they do not—and will not—interact with or interfere in human affairs. They are like scientists, observing our species; or voyeurs, if you like. The point is that their knowledge about what we do has no implications for us at all, unlike God's, who might mete out reward or punishment, whether in this life or the next. So, if participants still respond more quickly to affirm that The Ark know that *Joe cheats on his quizzes* than that *Hannah has 14 teeth*, then the moral bias about God's knowledge is just a general bias toward morally relevant content, rather than a bias about God's knowledge specifically.

Sixty-six participants completed this study, again from the University of Connecticut anthropology department. They attributed less omniscience to The Ark overall than believers did to God: The Ark knew a bit over 80% of the morally relevant and irrelevant things Ben asked about. More importantly, they did not respond more quickly to the morally relevant information than to the morally irrelevant information. As they did earlier, responses to The Ark's morally relevant knowledge took about 650 milliseconds, or about the same amount of time as they had in the previous study. Responses to morally irrelevant knowledge took just about 100 milliseconds more, which—according to Ben's statistical test—was a negligible difference: if there is general response bias in favor of morally relevant information, it is rather small.

But does this mean that God is *unique* where it comes to these perceptions of morally relevant and irrelevant knowledge? That's not what Ben thinks, with no offense intended toward the Almighty. The pattern we see with God should also be visible with any other super-knowing agent who is morally interested, who might reward good behavior and punish bad behavior. Orwellian watchers and Santa Claus come to mind, for example. So, Ben ran studies on these too.

There is, as far as I know, no doctrinal orthodoxy on the question of Santa Claus's omniscience. He obviously knows who has been naughty or nice, but his access to knowledge of other—nonmoral—things is not usually emphasized. This is reflected in Ben's sample of 50 participants: they only agreed that Santa knew morally irrelevant things about people 40% of the time, while almost always agreeing that Santa knew morally relevant things. People were also much quicker to respond to the questions about Santa's morally relevant knowledge than those about Santa's morally irrelevant knowledge: they took about 1,200 milliseconds for the latter questions, double the time for the former.

Ben also tried to invent a super-knowing moral supervisor that wasn't God, to see if that would do the trick. *NewLand*—a reference to *Newspeak*, the language of Oceania, Orwell's fictional totalitarian state in the novel *1984*—is a hyper-surveilling government in the year 2250, with high-resolution recording devices everywhere. There is no escaping NewLand's watch. Quite unlike The Ark, NewLand is very interested in intervening in human affairs: it rewards and punishes based on what it observes, which is everything. NewLand is rather like Justin Barrett's *Uncomp*, without the gloss of benevolence.

In contrast to Ben's findings about The Ark, this time participants did distinguish between morally relevant and morally irrelevant knowledge. On average, participants thought that NewLand had morally irrelevant knowledge about 80% of the time and morally relevant knowledge about 90% of the time. Furthermore, they responded more quickly for morally relevant information than for morally irrelevant information. In other words, participants treated NewLand—a morally concerned watcher, which they had just read about—rather like God.

Tuva or bust

So far, these studies show that people largely shaped by a Christian history and culture display a moralizing bias when thinking about God's knowledge. As I have said, however, it is a truism among scholars of religion that gods vary widely on how concerned they are with human affairs, as well as on what they are concerned about. For example, in some societies—sometimes called "animistic societies"—spiritual beings often take a *live and let live* approach to human beings, and only intervene when we encroach on their territory. Growing up in Malaysian Borneo, we were taught to behave respectfully in the forest lest we anger the tree spirits: this included the unforgettable instruction to ask for their permission before urinating in the woods. As far as anyone knew, they did not know or care about our lives in the city.

Gods and mortals also often enjoy transactional relationships, involving sacrifices and reciprocal acts of homage and patronage. Earlier, I mentioned that the gods of ancient Greek religion and East Asian religions are broadly unconcerned with what human beings do. The exception to this rule is in our direct dealings with them. Thus, votive offerings are left before statues of the Chinese *tudi gong* by petitioners who desire their protection and blessing. Christian saints arguably function in this way too: people do not tend to believe that St Jude is monitoring their behavior, but he can be appealed to in times of trouble, being the patron saint of lost causes. It is not just saints who can be persuaded to intervene in human affairs. The Greek gods could be too. The ancient Greeks could appeal to Zeus as Zeus *Horkios* to safeguard oaths or as Zeus *Xenios* to uphold norms of hospitality. Of course, there was no guarantee that he would care: the Greek gods are nothing if not capricious.

All the same, the moral focus of the God of the Abrahamic traditions should not be exaggerated, nor should our familiarity with ancient Greek religion lead us to assume that fickleness and moral fallibility is characteristic of gods outside of the moral monotheisms. Such a generalization would be woefully unwarranted without much more detailed evidence about the beliefs of people around the world. Since the research featured in this chapter, which was part of his doctoral research, Ben has dedicated much of his time and energy to collecting more cross-cultural evidence. So far, he has looked into over a dozen different societies around the world, focusing on remote places relatively free from the pervasive influence of the major religious traditions. I say *relatively* free because there are very few places left untouched by the so-called world religions, which include the Abrahamic religions, Buddhism, and Hinduism: such is the legacy of histories of war, colonialism, trade, and migration. In some places, however, the old traditions survive, albeit in modified form, alongside the newer, larger imports. This work has brought him and his colleagues to places like Hadzaland in Tanzania, the volcanic Tasawa islands of Fiji, and Ben's main doctoral field site, the Tyva Republic in southern Siberia.[6]

There are many ways in which an anthropologist might pick a field site. They might have a personal connection with the place: it might be where they lived for a while, where they grew up, or where their ancestors came from. Or they might have read about a place or a people previously studied, which has become the obvious context—the anthropological hotspot—for studying whatever phenomenon it is that they are interested in. Anthropologists fascinated by death rituals might head to Toraja in Indonesia; those interested in cargo cults might want to work in Papua New Guinea; those who want to investigate the evolution of language might try to study the Pirahã in the Brazilian Amazon; those who want to understand the contradictions of capitalism might set up in Lower Manhattan.

Ben discovered the Tyva Republic—Tuva, for short—from his interest in overtone singing, more commonly known as throat singing. This style is a way of manipulating your vocal cords to produce what sounds like two different pitches at the same time, as if you were whistling while singing. In Tuva, there is a practice of this style of singing. Ben's carpool buddies suggested that he seriously consider Tuva as a field site after he surprised them with a decent effort at throat singing on the way to work. It turned out to be perfect as it suited his academic interests as well!

Tuva is still a terrifically obscure place in Central Asia, in southern Siberia. The region has a rich history of religious practices, including what scholars call *Tengrism*—indigenous religious beliefs and practices with elements of animism, shamanism, and ancestor worship, as well as monotheism, the worship of the sky or sky god. Around the 16th century, Tibetan Buddhism became widespread in the area, though all religious practices became suppressed when the region fell under Soviet rule. After the fall of the Soviet Union, there had been a renaissance of indigenous culture, including Tengrism.

Some might argue that Tengrism isn't monotheistic, since it includes elements of animism. But I thoroughly approve of scholars' use of the term "monotheism" in this case, because it encourages us to reexamine monotheism in the context of the Abrahamic religions. After all, with thousands of saints and angels—not to mention our priests, who regularly invoke divine power in ritual contexts—Christianity cannot honestly be said to be rigidly monotheistic. From an anthropological perspective, the veneration of saints is not dissimilar to what we recognize in other traditions as ancestor worship; angels are not dissimilar to minor deities; priests are not dissimilar to shamans. If Christianity deserves to be called monotheistic, it is hard to see how Tengrism isn't.

As a remote area, Tuva is difficult to visit, though the fall of the Iron Curtain has certainly made it easier. Ben managed to make numerous visits, sometimes for months at a time, researching the moral functions of gods. The gods that interest Ben most in Tuva are *cher eeleri*—"masters of the place"—spirits in charge of things and places, like lakes and trees, familial land, and political jurisdictions. Tuvans do not believe *cher eeleri* to be morally concerned except within narrow domains: when Ben asked people what makes *cher eeleri* happy or angry, he found that they like rituals and offerings, and dislike the pollution and exploitation of their natural resources.[7] Like the gods of ancient Greek religions and the Bornean tree spirits of my childhood, *cher eeleri* did not seem very interested in what human beings do toward one another. This provided a neat contrast to God, as generally understood by anthropology undergraduates in New England: God cares about all manner of interpersonal behaviors. Tuva also provided an ideal test case of Ben's hypothesis against the conventional wisdom and scholarly consensus. Ben could ask Tuvans about what the local *cher eezi* (the singular form of *cher eeleri*) knows and cares about to see how far these gods' alleged moral apathy really goes. The *cher eeleri* are said to only care about rituals and their particular natural resources; therefore, we might expect their knowledge of morally relevant information to be quite limited, both geographically and in terms of domain. God cares and knows about dishonesty, theft and generosity, but *cher eeleri* allegedly do not.

This experiment dispensed with the reaction time stuff, opting for simpler technology.[8] The experiment was run in the United States as well as in Tuva. Eighty-eight Americans—all of whom said that they believed in an all-knowing God—completed questionnaires about what God knows. As in the previous experiment, these included morally relevant and morally irrelevant information about people. This time, some of the morally relevant behaviors occurred locally at the University of Connecticut, whereas others took place elsewhere. For example, participants were asked if God knows if *I told a lie to someone at the University of Connecticut?* and also if *I lied to someone when I was visiting friends in Russia?*

Similarly, 88 Tuvans were interviewed in the capital city of Kyzyl: Ben's team recruited people from all sorts of places, including schools and clinics, and even just on the streets. With the help of a translator, Tuvans were asked pretty much the same questions as the Americans, with a few modifications, mostly in place names. *Does the spirit-master know if I stole a car in Ak-Dovurak?* In both the United States and Tuva, participants were given five response options: "Of course," "Probably," "I don't know," "I doubt it," and "No." This allowed Ben to see how certain they were, and not just *whether* they thought God or the *cher eezi* knew something.

As expected, given the reaction time results, the Americans always responded "Probably" or "Of course" to questions about God's knowledge: they clearly believed in divine omniscience. However, their responses to the morally relevant and irrelevant knowledge differed, showing much more confidence about God's knowledge of morally relevant information than morally irrelevant information. Once again, Ben found cracks in people's commitments to divine omniscience. Although domain made a difference, location did not. The American participants were equally confident that God knew about things that happened on the university campus as about things that happened elsewhere.

The situation was rather different in Tuva. Tuvans were generally doubtful about the *cher eezi*'s morally irrelevant knowledge, about what one ate for breakfast yesterday and suchlike. They were less negative but still uncertain about the *cher eezi*'s knowledge of morally relevant behavior that takes place faraway, like stealing in St Petersburg. However, they thought that the *cher eezi* probably did know about morally relevant things that happened in its area, including things like lying and stealing. This is somewhat surprising, given Tuvans' stated theology. Furthermore, when Ben asked them what makes *cher eeleri* happy and angry, there was little indication from their answers to those questions that the spirits care about this kind of moral behavior at all. Perhaps then, this extended moralizing of *cher eeleri* minds is a sort of theologically incorrect intuition.

There are two possible explanations for this moralizing bias, and it will be up to future studies to test between them. The first possibility is that gods always serve some kind of moral policing function, even when this is not a part of their official repertoire. It is not just the so-called high gods who are morally concerned, but also *cher eeleri*, the gods of the Greek pantheon, and the tree spirits. Perhaps gods evolved to serve this function. The second possibility is that *minds* are always moral: if we cannot think of any minds without wondering what they know about our deeds and misdeeds, then it follows that we cannot think of *gods'* minds as being totally morally apathetic. The moralizing of gods' minds is, in this case, a byproduct of our general tendency to moralize all minds. Whatever the case, cultural forces—including the theological traditions we inhabit—can affect what morally relevant knowledge we attribute to the gods, but not omnipotently so. Under the right conditions, we can see our basic cognitive biases breaking through.

Psychology meets anthropology

This sort of thing is still quite rare, and we are only beginning to come up with a name for it. They call it *experimental anthropology* at the University of Connecticut, where Ben went to graduate school. Sometimes people say *cognitive anthropology* or *psychological anthropology*, but these emphasize the theoretical approaches rather than the research methods used. Field experiments—experiments conducted outside the laboratory—are not new as such, but the "field" in question has usually been the experimenter's backyard, the patch of the real world familiar to her.

However, studying in diverse fields encourages us to render the familiar strange too. With fresh eyes, we can detect elements in our traditions that we may not have noticed before: potential traces of animism, totemism, shamanism, and ancestor worship in religious traditions that officially repudiate them. Observing deep similarities underneath the more obvious differences across our religious traditions helps us see the fuller picture. Psychologists are interested both in differences between people and in their similarities, but I think it is our similarities that *really* get us excited. Those of us interested in how our brains and behavior have evolved over time see these similarities as the residues of our shared past.

In some ways, this idea of a shared psychology—the idea that despite differences in the color of our skin, the land we occupy, the languages we speak, the gods we worship, we have similar psychological pathologies that we inherited from our common ancestors—has discouraged cross-cultural research. After all, if we are all the same, what would be the point? But upon further examination, psychologists are beginning to realize that this is an antiscientific attitude. The only way to gain true scientific knowledge is to test, update, and refine our beliefs based on evidence we collect scientifically. Otherwise, we are operating on assumptions—and assumptions leave us open to bias and misinformation.

Galton's Problem

Cross-cultural research is important: it is also very difficult. It is particularly difficult if we want to explain similarities between cultures. When psychologists discover cross-cultural similarities, we are often tempted to conclude that we have discovered something about *human nature*, something basic and universal about human beings. But cultures are rarely independent: they borrow and learn from one another. As a result, similarities between cultures may stem from the universal structure of the human mind, or they may just be the result of some historical accident. This problem isn't a new one—it was first raised by Francis Galton in 1888; he of the correlations between prayer and longevity in Chapter 1—but it plagues us still.

An example from linguistics might be helpful here before we get to religion. The word for the number *two* in Malay is *dua*. In Paiwan, the language of the indigenous Taiwanese, it is *dusa*; in Malagasy, the national language of Madagascar, it is *roa*; in te reo Māori, it is *rua* as it also is in Easter Island's Rapa Nui over four thousand miles away. It is a remarkable coincidence that languages in Africa, Asia, and Australasia should be so similar. Or it would be, had human beings not invented sailing. Most experts think—based on linguistic as well as genetic evidence—that this Austronesian expansion began in Taiwan and spread to both Madagascar and the Polynesian islands via Southeast Asia over a period of over three thousand years.

Now consider the informal word for "mother" in Mandarin: *mama*. In Polish, it is *mama*; in Arabic, *mama*; in Russian, *mama*; in Quechua, *mama*; in Swahili, *mama*. In this case, the linguistic similarity probably has much less to do with cultural transmission than the fact that the *ma* sound is very easy for babies to make. The *ah* part does not require the baby to move its tongue or lips at all; and the *mm* happens when it closes its lips to pause before starting up again. Babies are just very likely to make a sound like *mama* very early on, which is also when they spend a lot of time with their mothers: so, mothers around the world may just have associated their babies' earliest sounds—*mama*, *ama*, *mam*, and other variants—with themselves. In other words, this linguistic similarity—unlike the case of the Austronesian word for the number two—is based on deep similarities in infant physiological development.

An analogous issue arises in the study of religion. It remains an open question, for example, whether Abrahamic, Hindu, and Tengrist beliefs in a supreme deity all evolved independently, or whether these cultural traditions have shaped one another's theologies. Galton's Problem grows as the world becomes more interconnected. Today, the Internet and increased access to air travel contribute to this. Even the people who self-identify as adherents of traditional indigenous religions are often reacting against foreign imports: we can see this in the Tengrist revival in central Asia, in the rehabilitation of *kastom* traditions in Melanesia; the growth of afro-Brazilian spiritism; and recent interest in British and European neopaganism. To complicate matters further, many people who describe themselves as members of a major world religion often also subscribe to beliefs from indigenous traditions. Thus, Tuvan Buddhists hold shamanic beliefs; Malaysian Muslims consult *bomohs* for health or fortune; and Ethiopian Christians carry talismans to protect them from the evil eye.

Challenges of cross-cultural measurement

Cultures mix when they meet, and they keep meeting. There may in fact be no way to tease apart shared psychology from shared history, but if there is, it involves doing research in very different places among very different peoples. Changes in global politics and technology have made this easier for many of us, but it has also made it more crucial that we check our biases, no matter how innocent.

Our measures need to be translated, and translation is a tricky business, prone to biases. A Pew Research Center poll in China from a few years ago reported that only 14% of the population thought that belief in God was necessary for morality. They then had to walk back this finding when it came to light that the word they used for "God"—*shangdi*, literally "highest emperor"—had strong Protestant connotations.[9] They were inadvertently asking participants if they believed the *Protestant* God was necessary for morality, which is an entirely different question. There are many words for God. Roman Catholics use *tianzhu* (sky/heaven lord). Some social scientists prefer *tian* (sky/heaven) to get away from the Christian connotations. In my own work, I have used *lao tianye* (old heaven elder)—and *tianshen* (heaven deity) to refer to God. It is not clear which one of these works best, though we all now know to avoid *shangdi*.

Beyond language barriers, our measures often need to adapt to cultural context. You may have noticed a shift in the way that Ben asked about *cher eeleri*'s knowledge in the second experiment from the way he asked about God's knowledge in the first experiment with the reaction times. In the first study, the questions were posed in the third person: *Does God know that Ann gives to the homeless?* In the second study, the questions all referred to the questioner: *Does the spirit-master know if I stole a car in Ak-Dovurak?* This change was precautionary. Names have cultural connotations—consider

Connor and Tyrone, which in an American context are clear social signals of ethnicity, White and Black respectively[10]—and social scientists use unfamiliar ones at our peril. Furthermore, hypothetical questions don't always play well in some cultural contexts; hypothetical questions involving fictional people might be additionally confusing.

We also need to be mindful of the difference between *measurements* and the *constructs* they purport to measure. Recall the difference between the Wechsler Adult Intelligence Scale (WAIS) and intelligence. Intelligence is the construct—the thing being measured, which might or might not exist—whereas the WAIS is a measure of intelligence, which might or might not be a good measure of intelligence. Crucially, WAIS might be a good measure of intelligence in one cultural context and a bad one in another: in other words, it might be culturally biased, as we discussed in Chapter 1. Analogously, the question "How often do you read the Bible?" might make sense as a part of a measure of how religious someone is in a Protestant context, but makes no sense whatsoever in a culture whose dominant religion does not involve sacred texts.

In addition, culture does not always refer to geographic locations or regional identity. The way psychologists and other social scientists ask questions might resonate with undergraduate students in psychology and anthropology departments, but the very same questions might sound odd to other people. Decades of relying on our own students as participants can impair our sensitivity to this. I have already mentioned the possibility that hypothetical questions involving fictional characters may be confusing. Psychologists have another common habit of asking the same question over and over again, slightly rephrased. We do this because repetition makes our measures more reliable. If, for example, an IQ test only consisted of a single question, and you happened to make a mistake on that one question, your test score would indicate that you were incredibly unintelligent, which might be unfair. Had I asked a bunch more questions, your careless mistake would be appropriately negligible. Ben too, in asking about God's knowledge, included multiple items in each category of things that God could know. But cross-cultural psychologists will tell you that people sometimes get fed up with being asked very similar questions one after another, and it is poor form to annoy one's participants.

Even technology can be a stumbling block. The Tuvans would have been fine working on computers, if Ben wanted to measure their reaction times as he did in the first experiment. But there are cultural contexts in which a laptop would be a novel sight and a significant distraction. The idea of a glowing screen presenting sentences for people to respond to by pushing keys on a keyboard would, in some such places, be utterly unfamiliar. In many places, mobile phones are more commonplace than personal computers, and might be more suitable. There are subtler examples too. Early on in my career, I received a phone call from my collaborators, who were on Tanna island in Vanuatu. We had designed an experiment that involved allocating money to themselves and one another, as a measure of cooperation. My collaborators sheepishly explained to me that the village they were brought to was quite ardently anti-Western, desiring to return to a traditional *kastom* way of life. One implication of this was that they rejected money as a foreign incursion.

"Can we do the experiment using salt instead?"

I didn't see why not, I replied, but I didn't know what the exchange rate was between *vatu* and salt.

I don't want to fetishize cross-cultural research in remote places like Tuva: nor do I want to exoticize the people who live quite differently from the way we do in what Joe Henrich charmingly dubbed Western, Educated, Industrialized, Rich, and Democratic—WEIRD—societies.[11] But there are various benefits of heading off to Tuva or Vanuatu or the Amazon, where religious traditions are not just the ones well-known to Western scholars: Judaism, Christianity, and Islam or even Buddhism and Hinduism. For starters, our knowledge is woefully incomplete if we omit belief systems unfamiliar to us, or people who live differently and far away from us. Restricting the psychology of religion to the major religious traditions would be a bit like the study of animal behavior being restricted to birds and mammals. (Incidentally, the study of animal behavior *is* very heavily biased toward birds and mammals.[12])

Of course, the study of the world religions is important: adherents to them make up most of the world's population, after all. We may well want to understand—from a psychological perspective—if there is anything about them that explains their success: or whether it is just a matter of historical contingency, missionaries convincing the right emperors at the right time. For a very long time animism, totemism, shamanism, and ancestor worship were widespread around the world, before the arrival of colonial missionaries. Even the Abrahamic monotheisms probably emerged out of polytheistic cultures. Grave goods—objects buried with the dead, like tools and jewelry—are among our earliest evidence for religion, tens if not hundreds of thousands of years ago. And as I suggested earlier, these beliefs and practices might still be around, and be more common than we think, hiding in plain sight among and coexisting with the major religions.

The upshot of all of this is that cross-cultural research is necessary but hard; or it is hard but necessary. It is a good job that people like Ben are trying to do more of it. In the early days of cross-cultural psychology, researchers were myopically focused on so-called individualist and collectivist cultures. This mostly entailed comparing Americans with Japanese people. Things have diversified since then, in part thanks to collaborations between psychologists and anthropologists. Long may this continue.

7

What makes an effective ritual?

Design: Within-subjects
Manipulate: Ritual characteristics
- presence or absence of characteristic
Measure: Efficacy
- self-report

Rituals and their efficacy

John Tillotson, the Archbishop of Canterbury from 1691 until his death in 1694, was no fan of transubstantiation: the idea that during the eucharist, bread and wine literally become the body and blood of Christ.[1] It remains the official teaching of the Roman Catholic Church today; however, a recent survey found that only a third of Roman Catholics in the United States agree with it.[2] Tillotson would probably have been pleased by this development, though it is unlikely that any Roman Catholics have recently read his book on the matter, *A Discourse Against Transubstantiation* published in 1684.

The book has been forgotten by most people, but for a single claim that still floats around the Internet. The then Dean of Canterbury Cathedral speculated that the phrase *hocus pocus*—already in the 17th century used in association with conjurors, and also jugglers—was a parodic corruption of words familiar to anyone who has been to a Roman Catholic Mass in Latin. It is a crucial moment, taken from the lips of Jesus himself at the Last Supper, and translated: *hoc est enim corpus meum*,[3] "for this is my body." These words are deemed nonnegotiable: they are necessary for the ritual to work, which also makes them the perfect target for satirical use by prestidigitators in the market for a clever incantation. That's what Tillotson figured, but there is no good evidence for this bit of amateur etymology.

Experimenting with Religion. Jonathan Jong, Oxford University Press. © Oxford University Press 2023.
DOI: 10.1093/oso/9780190875541.003.0007

This chapter is about when people believe that a ritual is effective. In Christian circles, this is called the question of a ritual's *validity*, which is an idea not dissimilar to the idea of the validity of a psychological measure, which we have discussed previously. A psychological measure is valid to the extent that it measures what is intended, like an IQ test measuring general intelligence. A ritual is valid to the extent that it accomplishes what is intended, whether it is a baptism, a marriage, or a eucharist. The point of a baptism ritual is to produce a baptized Christian. The point of a wedding is to join two individuals in matrimony. The point of a eucharistic liturgy is—though perhaps not for Tillotson—to bring the faithful into holy communion with Christ's real presence.

Rituals, like psychological measures, can fail at being valid, though this is probably where the analogy begins to break down. There is a lot that is conventional about psychometrics, but the reliability and validity of a psychological measure depends largely on independently observable phenomena. Anyone can challenge the reliability of an IQ test by showing that items within it are uncorrelated. Anyone can challenge the validity of an IQ test by showing that its scores have no predictive value whatsoever. Not so for rituals like baptism, eucharist, and marriage. The efficacy of a ritual is entirely socially stipulated. An authority decides what makes a ritual work, whether that authority is the Church, the state, or God. Some people are tempted to say that because rituals are social conventions they therefore don't have real effects. And I understand what they mean, but this view misses the prevalence and importance of social conventions in daily life.

Many things that affect our lives are real in a straightforwardly physical sense, like gravity or bacteria. But social facts govern our lives too, like laws and languages. Laws and languages are socially constructed—people make them up and accept them as "right" or "normal"—but it would be foolish to ignore them. Rituals are like that too. Whether or not you have been validly baptized or married can have a profound impact on your life. This is probably most obvious in the case of marriage. Not only in the eyes of religious authorities, but also according to secular laws in many countries, marriage comes with various rights and obligations. If a marriage ceremony didn't "work," you might lose those rights and be free from those obligations. Many a dispute about adultery and alimony and successions to crowns have depended on whether a marriage was validly celebrated. Just ask King Henry VIII, whose marital problems led to the split of the Church of England from that of Rome.[4]

Debates over the validity of various Christian rituals have gone on for centuries and continue still, both within and between Christian denominations. The Roman Catholic Church, for example, insists that the eucharist—or Mass—can only be validly presided over by a validly ordained priest. As it happens, this includes Eastern Orthodox priests. Unfortunately for me, the Anglican holy orders to which I belong have been repeatedly declared invalid in the eyes of the Roman See.[5] Having a validly ordained priest is not the only necessary criterion for a valid Mass. For a Mass to have taken place, the priest must also use the right words over the right material stuff. There is some flexibility over what constitutes the right words, but as we have seen, Jesus's words "this is my body" are considered essential, not only by Roman Catholics but by most Christians.[6]

As for matter, the material used for the Mass must be bread and wine: the bread must be made of wheat and without yeast, and the wine must be made of grapes and with no additives. This means, for example, that no valid Mass has been celebrated if Diet Coke and popcorn were used, even if it was presided over by a Roman Catholic priest using words from the Roman Missal. The Church has had to be quite creative to make provision for those who suffer from celiac disease or alcoholism. The bread may not be substituted with rice cakes or cornflakes, even for those who cannot consume gluten: instead, the bread can be made from wheat from which almost all the gluten has been removed. For alcoholics, the wine may not be substituted with regular grape juice: instead, *mustum* may be used, which is grape juice in which fermentation has begun and been suspended. Mustum typically contains less than 1% alcohol.[7] These strictures may seem impractical, and in a sense that is precisely the point: rituals are not intended to be convenient.

So far, these elements—the priest, the words, and the material substance— are all, as it were, external. But then there is the question of mental states, which is the focus of one of the most ancient debates about the validity of the Mass. In the early 4th century CE, Christians in the Roman Empire suffered severe persecution under the emperors Diocletian and Galerius. Christian gatherings were prohibited, clergy were imprisoned, churches were demolished, and scriptures and other sacred objects were destroyed or confiscated. Some Christians complied and cooperated with the authorities, surrendering their religious treasures, perhaps to protect themselves or others. They came to be called *traditores*—literally, those who have handed over, from which we get both the words "traitor" and "tradition"—and some Christians distrusted them when the persecution was over.

Not only were the *traditores* distrusted, but the priests among them were deemed invalid and therefore unable to preside over a valid Mass. This led to a schism, particularly within the Church in Carthage in modern day Tunisia. The *Donatists*—named for Donatus Magnus, a bishop who was one of the movement's leaders—insisted that *traditores* needed to be rebaptized and reordained if they were to resume their religious functions. This view flourished for a little while in a few places, but ultimately lost out to the current orthodoxy that a Christian's baptism and ordination are indelible. Even if surrendering holy things to pagan rulers was sinful, to commit such a sin would not invalidate one's baptism or ordination. And as long as someone has been validly ordained, they can validly preside over a Mass. The validity of the Mass turns on the ordination of the priest, not on what he has done since or even on his *character* now. Sinners can celebrate the Mass.

Over time, this view that the priest's character did not threaten the validity of the Mass was expanded to cover psychological states more generally. This meant that the validity of the Mass did not depend on whether the priest was having a bad day or even a crisis of faith: the laity could rest assured that they were participating in a valid Mass. When I first discovered this quirk of Roman Catholic sacramental theology, I brought it up with Gregory Dawes, one of my doctoral advisors, a New Testament scholar and philosopher who was a Jesuit priest who had long since lost his faith. He had himself excommunicated, quit his job as a priest, and eventually got married and started a beautiful family. As an undergraduate student in his philosophy of religion class, I admired his honesty, humor, rigor, and clarity of thought. It was quite unusual to do a doctorate in psychology partly supervised by a philosopher, but I was eager to learn more from Greg. I also asked him whether he would administer the last rites to me if he happened to be around in my final moments. This would involve him administering the eucharist, hearing my confession, and anointing me with holy oil, the latter two of which may only be done by a priest. Greg was validly ordained, even though he had lost his faith and been excommunicated: so, his actions would be valid, as long as he intended to do what the Church does in performing these actions. They would be *illicit*—contrary to canon law—but they would "work." Bemused, Greg agreed.

So, intentions do matter, but only in a very minimal way. All Greg has to intend is to do what the Church does in hearing my confession and pronouncing absolution, and in anointing me with oil. Greg would not have to believe in the efficacy of the prayers and rituals involved. This is like that probably apocryphal story usually told about the physicist Niels Bohr. When a visitor to his house noticed a horseshoe hanging on a wall and asked if he believed in such things. Bohr replied in the negative, adding that as he understood it, it would bring him good luck whether he believed in it or not.

Perhaps it is odd to talk about intending to "do what the Church does," but an additional example and counterexample might help. Consider that you are stranded and mortally injured in the wilderness with a friend, who happens to be an atheist. As you lay dying, you ask a favor of your friend, that she fetches water from a nearby stream to baptize you, saying the words "I baptize you in the name of the Father and of the Son and of the Holy Spirit," as is required by the Roman Catholic Church and many others. The only two requirements for baptism are the use of water and this formula of words: the person doing the baptizing need not be a priest, nor even a Christian. Your friend does not believe that baptism does anything, nor does she really know what the Roman Catholic Church teaches on the matter. But so long as she intends to do whatever it is the Church thinks it does in baptism, your baptism would be valid. Now, consider a very similar example, but where you are making a film in the wilderness with a friend, and the film includes a baptism scene. While she is pouring the water on you and saying the requisite words, she has no intention to baptize you: rather, her intention is to *pretend* to baptize you. In this case, no baptism would have taken place, even though all the external requirements had been met. Many Christians would probably be unwilling to act out the scene in this manner anyway, but there is nothing doctrinal standing in their way.

There is one more thing to notice about Christian liturgy before we move on. Observant Catholics might notice that the requirements for the validity of the eucharist or baptism are quite minimal compared to what actually happens in churches on Sunday. In practice, there seem to be a lot of rules. There are rules about what the priest wears, for example, and about the gestures he makes. The sign of the cross is always made with his right hand, from top to bottom and his left to his right. He hovers his hands above the bread and wine when he invokes the Holy Spirit. At masses all over the world, priests bow and genuflect at the same points of the liturgy. Deviations from this pattern are rare and are frowned upon, despite the fact that they do not *invalidate* the ritual.

From sacraments to *simpatias*

So far, I have not tried to define "ritual": rather, I have provided examples from a specific religious tradition, which may be familiar to you. The academic literature is replete with proposed definitions, none of which are uncontroversial: the same is true for "religion," which is also why I have avoided defining that. What I will say is that—for the purposes of this chapter—rituals are acts that aim to accomplish some outcome, but for which the means of working are mysterious.

Take the case of the eucharist, for example. The Church insists that the eucharistic elements must be bread and wine. But there is, as far as we know, nothing about the physical and chemical structures of bread and wine that make them especially amenable to being transubstantiated. If pushed, we would say that it has to be bread and wine because that is what Jesus used at his Last Supper. In other words, we are obeying precedence. This is also why no substitute is possible. Compare this to how we think about ingredients in a recipe. The ingredients in a recipe are what they are because something about their taste and texture contributes to the dish: and ingredients are therefore substitutable by things with similar taste and texture.

Speaking of recipes, let's consider *simpatias*—sometimes translated "charms"—a type of ritual prevalent in Brazil, which is the main object of the experiments in this chapter. Simpatias often sound like recipes:

Put a spoonful of honey in a cup. Then fill it with mineral water. Mix well. Now, take a piece of paper and write the person's name on it. Put the paper in the cup to soak in the honey and water for twenty-four hours. Then remove the paper and drink four large sips of the mixture. At each sip, say "[Person's name], you are mine; I am yours." Repeat every day for a week.[8]

On the night of a full moon, remove seven strong and healthy hairs from your head. Do not use hairs that have already fallen out. Holding the hair in the moonlight, say aloud "May my hair grow strong and healthy as the energy of this moon has power over nature." Then leave the hair directly exposed to the moonlight overnight. The next day, bury the hair in a place that only you know. Drizzle the ground with oil or milk. Repeat every day for a week, with prayers to the Blessed Virgin Mary.[9]

On a piece of yellow paper, write the word "money" only once. Fold the piece of paper several times, until it is very small. Place the folded piece of paper in the middle of a piece of yellow fabric. Place some bay leaves there too. Fold the fabric so that the paper and bay leaves are enclosed. Now, keep this in your wallet or purse to attract money.[10]

There are simpatias for all kinds of things, as the examples show: simpatias for your love life, for your career and prosperity, and for your health and protection. Pamphlets of simpatias can be picked up in supermarkets and other public places. There are also many websites full of them, categorized by function, from which I found these examples. Brazilians seem to take simpatias seriously, at least more seriously than Niels Bohr took his horseshoe and more seriously than people in Britain usually take familiar actions like knocking on wood, crossing fingers, and tossing coins into fountains.

Lab-made simpatias

One of the examples that André Souza gave to Cristine Legare when they first spoke about simpatias was surprisingly familiar to me. When he was growing up in Brazil, his mother used to have him sleep with a dictionary tucked under his pillow, to help him with schoolwork. I never did this as a child, but my friends and I used to joke about it all the time, saying that we could absorb knowledge from our textbooks by osmosis. For us, it was an absurd and hilarious proposition: not so for André's mother. She now points out that it worked, of course. André ended up in graduate school at the University of Texas in Austin, where he met Cristine, then new to the faculty. He has since taught at the University of Alabama, which he left for a successful career in the tech industry, working at Google and Facebook. Who knows if any of that would have happened were it not for the dictionary under his pillow?

Cristine wanted to run experiments on simpatias: not to see whether they actually work, but to see why people believe that they do. Very much like Deb Kelemen, Cristine started her career studying how children think about causes, including the causes of health and illness. As a doctoral student at the University of Michigan, she had run studies in South Africa about the coexistence of biomedical and witchcraft-based causal explanations of disease.[11] Simpatias, often used to treat ailments as well as heartbreak and hair loss, were right up her alley. So André wrote to his mother, asking her to send him a stack of pamphlets. This immediately worried her: what problems were plaguing André in Texas such that he needed *stacks* of simpatias?

Reading through the dozens and dozens of simpatias from books, magazines, and websites, Cristine and André tried to detect patterns, but all they saw at first was unmanageable diversity. In the three examples I gave above, the words—said or written—make it clear what each simpatia is for. The use of hair was a decent clue too. But most of the objects used in simpatias seem unconnected to their purpose, and often appear in very different kinds of simpatias. Bay leaves, for example, are not only for attracting wealth, but also for speeding up divorce proceedings. Honey appears in simpatias for lawsuits, as well as those for romance. Even hair, obviously involved in trichological simpatias, also appears in simpatia pregnancy tests.

After hours and hours of reading, tagging, and categorizing simpatias, covering her office floor with sticky notes, Cristine and André finally decided to focus on *nine* characteristics of simpatias. Some of their simpatias specified a time or place for them to be performed; others didn't. Some of them were very specific about the materials used; others weren't. Some of them involved many steps or a lot of repetition: others were simpler and shorter. Some required many objects: others fewer. Some of the objects were edible, and sometimes they had to be eaten: not so in other cases. Sometimes a religious icon—like an image of a Christian saint—was involved: sometimes not. Maybe the absence or presence of these characteristics was significant in some way.

With these nine characteristics in mind, they began composing their own simpatias, a pair for each trait. For example, they wrote up one simpatia that specified time:

> In the first day of the last quarter phase of the moon, take the milk from a coconut and give it to the affected person to drink. After that, ask the person to spit three times in the hole made in the coconut. Following this, light a brand-new white candle and drop the wax around the hole until the hole is sealed. Take the coconut to a faraway beach or river.

And they had another version that did not specify time, omitting the first part of the first sentence. Similarly, in one case, they specified where the material had to come from:

> Collect seven red apples directly from an apple tree. In the morning, before eating anything, peel the apples, eat them and save the peel. Right before going to bed, make a tea with the peel.

And in the other version, they only said to "purchase seven red apples," without saying where from. So it went for all nine pairs of simpatias: within each pair, the simpatias were identical but for a single characteristic. This would allow Cristine and André to see which, if any, of the characteristics affected people's judgments about whether the simpatias would work. Perhaps having a religious icon boosts people's confidence: perhaps not. Perhaps specifying when the simpatia had to be performed would make a difference: perhaps not. They could now find out. Before that, however, they wanted to know what Brazilians thought of the simpatias they had just invented. They needed to make sure that their simpatias were recognizable as simpatias before they could go any further. They needed to go to Brazil.

Fieldwork in Brazil

It is much easier to get to Belo Horizonte in southeastern Brazil than it is to get to Tuva. André's journey to graduate school in the United States is more remarkable than his trips back to run these experiments. He grew up in the slums of Belo Horizonte, moving house whenever their family was evicted, sometimes doing homework by candlelight when they couldn't afford the electricity bill. He had even been deported from his first visit to the United States as an exchange student: he needed to work to afford living costs, but this violated the terms of the program. Despite all this, he made it back and has made a good life there. I'm a sucker for good immigrant stories.

The city runs public health centers called *Posto de Saúde* to serve local communities' simple medical needs: cuts and grazes, aches and pains, not life-threatening emergencies. Demand for treatment is high, and people often wait in line to be seen. This presented André and Cristine with captive audiences, perfect for recruiting participants and collecting data. Socialized medicine turns out to be good for science, among its other societal benefits. You might think that a medical facility would be a bad place for recruiting simpatia users: simpatias and modern medicine do not seem the most compatible of bedfellows. And yet, Brazilians are perfectly happy to use folk remedies alongside modern medicine. They are not peculiar on this note: the coexistence of folk and scientific medicine is fairly common around the world. It should even be familiar in the West, where most evangelical Christians rely on prayer as well as on pills.

For their first study, André recruited 60 adult participants in Belo Horizonte, and showed them each nine of their simpatias, one from each trait pair. They specifically wanted to know whether Brazilians familiar with simpatias had intuitions that they lacked, about how the forms of the rituals matched their functions. To figure this out, they asked participants to match each of the nine simpatias to one of 18 possible problems that simpatias are commonly used to solve like bad luck in love, unemployment, toothaches, and sadness. Participants were to choose the problem each simpatia would be most effective for, but they could also say that the simpatia was good for nothing.

The Brazilian participants did not agree at all on how simpatias matched with problems: even the most consistently matched pairs were chosen less than 3% of the time. Cristine and André were rather encouraged by this. It meant that they weren't just missing something obvious when they saw no patterns earlier. They were also very pleased by the participants who claimed to have used some of their simpatias before, despite the fact that they had made them up. This was all the proof they needed that they had done a decent job creating experimental stimuli. The next study was the real test to see which—if any—of the nine characteristics they identified affected people's judgments of how well simpatias worked.

This time they recruited 80 Brazilians, again from public clinics in Belo Horizonte, again showing them nine of the simpatias, one randomly chosen from each pair. For each pair of simpatias, roughly 40 participants saw the version with the characteristic present (e.g., time specified) and roughly 40 saw the version with the characteristic absent (e.g., time unspecified). This allowed Cristine and André to compare *within* each pair, to see which characteristics affected what participants thought of the simpatias. As the first study showed no obvious correspondence between the form of the simpatia and its perceived function, Cristine and André randomly matched simpatias to problems before showing them to the participants. All the participants had to do now was to say how effective they thought the simpatia might be for that problem, on a scale of 1 to 10, with the higher values indicating *less* confidence that the simpatia would work. Had I designed the study, higher values would indicate more confidence in the simpatia, but no one asked me.

Generally speaking, the participants were not very optimistic about the efficacy of Cristine and André's simpatias: even those who used simpatias in real life tended to be on the fence about whether these ones would work. It is hard to know whether this reflects a broader skepticism toward simpatias, or whether these invented simpatias were just less persuasive than ones already known to the participants. There's nothing unusual about doing something despite being skeptical of its efficacy. People who knock on wood, cross their fingers, or throw coins in fountains would probably not say that they were very confident that these actions would work to produce the desired outcomes. Even people who pray might not say that praying for something significantly increases the probability of it happening. Sometimes we do things *just in case* they work, not because we are confident that they will. This extends far beyond superstitious, magical, or religious acts. When I turn a computer off and on again to fix a problem, it is not because I believe that it will but because I hope that it might.

Anyway, the point of the experiment is not to see how good Cristine and André are at making people believe in simpatias. It is to see what makes the difference between simpatias that are seen as more effective and those that are seen as less effective. They found that the presence of a religious icon made no difference. Neither did the edibility of the material, nor instructions to actually eat the material, affect perceptions of efficacy. The number of items involved—say, just a piece of clothing versus a piece of clothing plus a personal object plus a shoe—also made no difference. Specificity about where to perform the simpatia and where the items came from also had no impact. However, simpatias were perceived as more effective when time was specified, when there were more steps involved, and when the instructions said to repeat the procedure multiple times.

This too was very satisfying, but there was more work to be done. In this experiment, Cristine and André only had one pair of simpatias for each of the characteristics they looked at. It is possible that their findings were just artifacts of those particular simpatias. If so, it would be misleading to draw broader conclusions. Take, for example, the specificity of material: in this study, they found that specifying where the material came from did not affect participants' efficacy judgments. But it would be premature to infer from this that specifications about the material are generally irrelevant. What if, instead of specifying where the apples were from, they specified the *type* of apple required? In both simpatias in that pair, Cristine and André specified the color and number of apples. What if they had left these unspecified in one of them? Would people respond differently to the two simpatias then? If so, this would show that specifying the materials does matter, even if specifying where to get them does not. This result would have been a sort of *false negative*, a failure to detect a difference where there was one. There could also be false positives. Participants found the coconut milk simpatia more effective when the instructions specified performing the simpatia during the first day of the last quarter phase of the moon. Perhaps it was not the specificity of the time per se that made the difference, but the mention of the moon, which is a common motif in simpatias.

Cristine and André were, quite understandably, more worried about false positives than false negatives. In their next experiment, they dropped almost all the characteristics that seemed to make no difference, like the specificity of materials. Even now, Cristine thinks that it's a promising characteristic to re-examine, but they decided to focus on the characteristics that did show some promise, to check that the initial findings weren't just flukes. This is a conservative move, which is usually a prudent one in science. The only other characteristic they retained was the presence or absence of religious icons. Given the influence of Roman Catholicism in Brazil, it does seem surprising for religious icons to make no difference, even if simpatias are not exactly encouraged by the Vatican. Maybe they found no difference because they specified the wrong saint for the problem in question. After all, Roman Catholicism admits many specific patron saints. This next experiment clearly needed more simpatias, and so Cristine and André drafted more so that they had three pairs of simpatias for each of the four characteristics: the three that made a difference earlier, plus icons.

They recruited another 22 participants, again from public clinics in Belo Horizonte. Having observed earlier that some Brazilians believed in simpatias more than others, they specifically recruited participants who use simpatias regularly and broadly believe that they work. Every participant was shown 12 simpatias, one from each pair. As before, participants were told what problem each simpatia was meant to solve. All they had to do was to rate how well they thought each simpatia would work. To their relief, they replicated their previous findings on specifying time, increased number of steps, and instructions to repeat the ritual. They also found that, this time, the presence of a religious icon did increase participants' confidence that the simpatia would work. They were reluctant to speculate about why the religious icon made a difference in this experiment and not the previous one, but I have a guess. In the earlier study, they specified an icon of the Virgin Mary in the simpatia, but Mary is a fairly broad-based sort of saint. This study now included a simpatia for wealth that invoked São Expedito, who is considered the patron saint of merchants, and another simpatia against unemployment that involved St Edwiges, who is celebrated by Brazilians as the patron saint to debtors. The specific pairings of these saints to those problems may have done the trick.

Simpatias in America

The next experiment Cristine and André ran was a little surprising to me: they brought the simpatias back to the United States, to show them to undergraduate students there. They expected these American students to disbelieve in simpatias; what they wanted to know was whether the same characteristics that affected perceptions of efficacy in Brazil would have the same effect in America. The Americans might not believe that the simpatias worked, but perhaps they would nevertheless be *more* willing to think they worked when a religious icon was involved, when time was specified, and when the simpatia involved more steps and more repetition.

This move, to bring the simpatias to the United States, reveals something about how Cristine and André understand about how people think about rituals. From the outside, rituals like simpatias often look very odd, very different from the normal ways in which we negotiate the physical world. No matter how simpatias are believed to bring about their intended effects, the mechanism of actions seems very different from that of ordinary actions. We typically have some idea of how our actions might bring about outcomes. If we are depressed, we might take pills because we think they will do something to our brain chemistry, which will in turn affect our mental health. If we feel unattractive, we might try to improve our appearance by dieting, exercising, or buying new clothes, on the theory that fit, thin, well-dressed people are seen as more attractive in our culture. If we hate our jobs, we might spruce up our résumés, with the thought that potential employers might be impressed by what we put on them. In each of these cases, we might be wrong about how things work, but we have some intuitive ideas about them.

Simpatias are more mysterious. How is drinking diluted honey meant to help with our love lives? How is moonlight supposed to promote hair growth? How does a bay leaf attract wealth? Cristine and André could see as well as anybody else that simpatias are rather different from other actions that are meant to affect the world in some way. But they also had the hunch that people apply some of the same principles to simpatias that they do to thinking about other causes and effects. They thought about how things like repetition and temporal specificity come into play in our daily lives in other ways. Health-related behaviors seem to be rife with these kinds of specificity. Medicines, for example, often come with clear instructions about when they are to be taken and how often, and patients rarely have any idea why, even if their physicians might. Similarly, the instructions for cardiopulmonary resuscitation (CPR) are very precise: these days, we are told to give 30 chest compressions follows by 2 breaths, and then to repeat until the ambulance arrives. A decade ago, it was 15 compressions and 2 breaths. There have been other recent changes to CPR too, about the speed and force applied and even about the order in which to do things. The ABC—airway-breathing-circulation—that I was first taught over a decade ago has since been rearranged to CAB. Those of us trained in first aid will probably try to comply to these new guidelines, but very few of us will know what the new evidence is for this change, or even whether such evidence exists. Exercise regimes are also typically quite rigid. Push-ups, abdominal crunches, and barbell curls all have to be performed just so, with a specific number of sets and repetitions, and with breaks of exact durations between each set. Here too, people rarely know the reasons behind the instructions. But we follow them. And maybe we follow them *because* specificity and repetition confers on them the sheen of efficacy.

Cristine and André's hunch was that we all share intuitions about what makes for effective actions, and that we apply these intuitions for things like simpatias as well as things like CPR. If so, then even Americans who don't know much about and certainly do not believe in simpatias will still judge those that involve more specificity and repetition as being more effective. So, they translated their 12 pairs of simpatias into English and attempted to replicate the study among 68 American undergraduates. This experiment was basically identical to the one in Belo Horizonte, except that the whole thing was done via computers rather than face-to-face. As expected, American undergraduates were much more skeptical of simpatias than the Brazilians were. But like the Brazilians—though to a much lesser extent—they were more optimistic about the simpatias working when they required more steps and more repetition, and when a religious icon was present. Specifying the time when the simpatia should be performed made no difference.

Frankly, I am surprised that Cristine and André managed to replicate any of their Brazilian findings. It is, as we have already noted, logically possible to disbelieve in a simpatia less under some conditions than others, but I would still have expected the American undergraduates to dismiss all the simpatias indiscriminately, regardless of how much repetition and specificity they involved. It is true that the American participants were quite dismissive: efficacy ratings hovered around 8 on the 10-point scale, with 10 being the lowest level of perceived efficacy. The differences between groups were very small, about half a point within each pair. It is entirely possible that the finding would not replicate if we re-ran the experiment with a much larger sample. Someone should do that.

Ecological validity

One of my great worries about experimental psychology is the lack of what we call *ecological validity*. There is something obviously artificial about the laboratory setting. People can be religious anywhere, but they tend to do so in churches and temples, and perhaps in their homes. We should not be too quick to assume that the religiosity that we can measure in the laboratory is the same sort of thing as the religiosity that we can observe at Friday prayers at the mosque. Similarly—and perhaps more significantly—our experimental materials rarely bear any resemblance to actual accoutrements of religious devotion. In none of the experiments covered in this book so far have researchers observed Roman Catholics praying from breviaries or Hindus chanting mantras or Muslims performing *raka'at* or Buddhists handling *mala* beads. Instead, they have designed puppet shows about dead mice and vignettes about God doing crossword puzzles. It is totally understandable that they have done so. The ability to control the minutiae of our experimental stimuli is what allows us to make the comparisons and causal inferences we want to make. Real religious material is too messy for our purposes.

This is what stands out about Cristine and André's experiments, and perhaps it is a peculiarity of the phenomenon they chose to study. They directly examined how people think about simpatias. It's true that they made up the simpatias, but simpatias are very amenable to being made up. This element of Brazilian folk practice is fluid, quite unlike the creeds, scriptures, and rituals of the world religions. In this, they are like horoscopes or—to pivot out of the supernatural altogether—like jokes. In each of these cases, the genre provides a structure, but the content is malleable. This combination of easily recognizable structure and malleable content lends simpatias—and horoscopes and jokes—to be studied experimentally. We can have both ecological validity and experimental control.

Cristine worries that psychology has become too abstract, too distant from the real life behaviors that our theories purportedly aim to explain. Psychologists wring their hands a lot about issues of definition and measurement, and we continue to argue over the reliability and validity of our tools, our IQ tests, questionnaires, and implicit measures. But all this is for nought if we forget that the point of measuring these psychological constructs— religiosity, intelligence, anxiety, or whatever—is to help us understand the things that ordinary human beings do in temples and at home and in hospitals and at school. We want to understand why people pray and how they solve problems and how they cope with illness and grief. So, if we never actually observe people praying, solving problems, coping with stuff, then we run the risk of having gone astray. Cristine wanted to know how people used simpatias, and so she used simpatias in her experiments. She started here, with a particular kind of ritual, rather than with rituals in some vague and abstract sense. It seems like an obvious thing to do, but it is surprisingly rare.

There is cause for optimism in the growing closeness between anthropology and psychology. Cristine and André are not the only researchers taking the tools of experimental psychology out of the lab, equipped with a rich background knowledge of the local cultural context. Ben Purzycki studied Tuvan beliefs about *cher eeleri* compared to American beliefs about God. Before them, Tanya Luhrmann had conducted both ethnographic and quantitative psychology work among American evangelicals, to figure out what was going on when they claimed to talk to God.[12] Justin Barrett's vignette studies can also be seen as efforts to figure out how Christians—and in later studies, Hindus—understand divine attributes in the course of very normal religious behavior: the reading and hearing of stories. None of these other studies include stimuli like Cristine and André's,—designed to mimic things being used in the real world—but they do share the virtue of closely examining specific manifestations of religious or supernatural belief.

8

Does death anxiety drive religion?

Design: Between-subjects
Manipulate: Death thoughts v. control
- write about death v. TV
Measure: Supernatural beliefs
- self-report & implicit

In the space below, jot down, as specifically as you can, what you think will happen to you physically as you die and once you are physically dead.

Death really begins before death. Or, put another way, there are multiple criteria for what counts as death, even if we limit ourselves to medical definitions. There is, for example, *whole brain death*, which also turns off all other physiological functions. Or there is *higher brain death*, which is the irreversible cessation of consciousness even while basic physiological processes—heartbeat, breathing—remain more-or-less intact. Or there is *cardiopulmonary death*, which is when the heart and lungs stop working by themselves, though there might still be some brain activity. The heart, lungs, and different brain regions do not always all suddenly stop working at the same time. And before one or all of them stop working, some of our other organs may have already begun to fail and die.

But you were asking about *me*. Statistically speaking, I guess I will probably die lying in a hospital or hospice bed, though I would really prefer to be in my own home at the end. I will likely be about 86 years old, based on data collected by the United Kingdom's Office of National Statistics.[1] I might have dementia, which affects about one in six individuals above the age of 80. I imagine that I'll feel it coming, maybe even smell it coming: some people say that there's a scent, released by our already decaying cells. Most people, especially men, die of heart failure, so I suppose I might feel a tightness in my chest before I die. I hope there'll be some kind of euphoric sensation: some researchers say that near-death experiences are a bit like a ketamine trip.

Experimenting with Religion. Jonathan Jong, Oxford University Press. © Oxford University Press 2023.
DOI: 10.1093/oso/9780190875541.003.0008

But you want to know what I think will *physically* happen, so I should probably stick to that. My heart will stop, I'll gasp, and then fall still and silent. Pretty much immediately—within four minutes, they say—decomposition kicks in. My enzymes, previously helpful chemicals, now begin digesting me from the inside. All the bacteria that live in me—my *gut microflora*; such a pretty name—also start eating me and spreading outside my digestive tract throughout my body: they roam unchecked by my immune system, now no longer functioning. The carbon dioxide inside me can no longer escape in the usual way, so levels of carbonic acid begin to rise, which causes more and more cells to rupture. *Pallor mortis* begins within three hours, peaking at the twelfth.

> In addition to the physical description, write in some detail about the feelings that the thoughts of your own dying arouse in you.

Gosh. It's funny: I guess I had been imagining my own death as if I was *watching* it from the outside. So it felt quite clinical, really. But that can't be right. I wouldn't say that I've been feeling scared or anxious while answering the previous question. There have been times when thinking about death has scared me too. Thinking about my mother's death used to send me into mild panic. I really did not like that: it's best I don't dwell too much on that now, actually. I did have this revelation when I was maybe 15, that the world was spinning around fine without me long before I was born and would probably do so long after I was dead. That was not a nice thought. Anyway, these days I feel a pang of sadness every so often, thinking about how much I will miss everything when I die: my wife, especially. We are newly married. But maybe I won't miss anything at all, what with being dead and all. I don't know. It's all a little unsettling.

Terror management theory

Since the late 1980s, a growing group of social psychologists have been asking participants to think and write about their deaths, to see how that would affect them psychologically. It seems like a cruel thing to do, but people rarely feel too distressed by the task. I have run this sort of study a few times now, and only *once* did anyone break into tears. Completing the task myself, as I have just done, was sobering, but not upsetting. But we are getting ahead of ourselves.

Social psychologists commonly draw a distinction between *cognitive* explanations on one hand and *motivational* ones on the other. The difference between the two is fuzzy, but useful. Roughly speaking, a cognitive explanation of a psychological phenomenon is one that refers to people's abilities or tendencies to perceive and process information. Most of the experiments we have looked at have tested cognitive hypotheses: analytic thinking, teleology, anthropomorphism, dualism, and causal reasoning biases are all cognitive factors.

In contrast, a motivational explanation is one that refers to people's psychological needs or desires. Often these are unexpressed, subconsciously affecting our behavior. The idea—made popular by Sigmund Freud—that religion is secretly a form of *wish-fulfillment*, is a classic example of a motivational theory of religion. He thought that religious beliefs resulted from unconscious guilt and fear. Of course, we do not necessarily have to choose between cognitive and motivational theories: it is almost always the case in psychology that both kinds of factors have roles to play. All the same, it was always the latter that grabbed my attention as an undergraduate: there was something delightfully subversive about the idea that we are motivated by a morass of unconscious desires.

At the end of my undergraduate studies around 2008, I had decided to focus on the motivational causes of religious belief, and so I scribbled down a list of potential motivations. It was something like:

Fear of death
Need for perceived control
Need to believe in a just world
Fear of loneliness
Need for self-esteem
Need to explain phenomena

The plan—hilariously naïve in retrospect—was to investigate *every* item on the list over the course of the three standard years of a New Zealand doctoral program. A decade later, I have still not quite gone beyond the first item on the list, though other people have covered some of this ground.[2]

The year I left New Zealand—2012—was an eventful one for my field of research. Just a few months after those three papers about analytic thinking and religiosity covered in Chapter 2 were published, another triplet emerged, all three reporting experiments about death and religion, and all three focusing on *non*believers in one way or another. This chapter tells the story of two of them, one by Kenneth Vail at the University of Missouri at the time, and the other by myself, just arrived at Oxford from the University of Otago in New Zealand.[3] Perhaps it is self-indulgent to end this book with a critical reevaluation of my own work. On the other hand, it seems a shame not to revisit my early attempts at experimental psychology, armed with the lessons learned from the other studies we have already looked at in previous chapters. More than eight thousand miles apart, and in mutual ignorance of one another, Ken and I had both been asking the same questions, and even starting from the same theory, which must possess the most melodramatic name in any branch of science: Terror Management Theory.

Terror Management Theory is the brainchild of Sheldon Solomon, Jeff Greenberg, and Tom Pyszczynski, who met as graduate students at the University of Kansas in the late 1970s. Like me, they were interested in the fundamental motivations behind human behavior. Together they stumbled across a proposal almost too audacious to be true, in a book called *The Denial of Death* by an American cultural anthropologist, Ernest Becker. The book was published in 1973, toward the end of the wave of scholarly attention to death that included Jessica Mitford's scathing indictment of the American funeral industry in 1963, Elisabeth Kübler-Ross's still ubiquitous work on the stages of grief in 1969, and Philip Ariès's critical historical narrative of the West's conception of death in 1974. Becker described the book as his "first mature work," but it was also to be his final book published before his death in March 1974, aged 49 years: just two months later, it won the Pulitzer Prize for Nonfiction.

In Kübler-Ross's famous model, based on her clinical experience with terminally ill patients, denial is just the first stage of coping with our own imminent death, the others being anger, bargaining, depression, and acceptance.[4] Becker's rejoinder is that we are always, all of us, denying our mortality, either by distraction or by displacement. Almost everything we do—every individual and cultural activity and achievement, praying or painting, raising children or empires—is unconsciously and obliquely an attempt to obtain immortality, whether literal or symbolic. It is not uncommon to hear talk of people "living on" through their work or "living vicariously" through their children: from Becker's point of view, these metaphors reveal our motivations. These are, of course, means of obtaining *symbolic* immortality, in contrast to endeavors to extend our biological lives or to guarantee our postmortem survival. Examples of the latter endeavors are easy to conjure. Any number of kings and oligarchs have tried to evade death by means of elusive elixirs or the extension of telomeres; any number of folk from all societal strata have hoped in karma or the favor of the gods, in whose gift is life everlasting.

When they first started out, Jeff, Tom, and Sheldon were not much interested in literal immortality: it would be a while before any Terror Management theorists turned their attention there. Like so many social psychologists at the time, they were caught up in the effort to understand *self-esteem*, and the apparent need we have for feeling good about ourselves. Researchers were discovering all sorts of things about how self-esteem contributes to mental health and other desirable outcomes, and about the lengths to which we often go to maintain positive self-evaluations. What Jeff, Tom, and Sheldon wanted to know was *why* self-esteem was so important to us, and they thought that Ernest Becker's ideas might have given them the answer.

The theory as it has been developed and elaborated over the years is complicated, but at a basic level it begins with the simple observation that we—perhaps alone among animals—are aware of our mortality, the certain fragility and possible futility of our existence. It then asserts that this truth is too awful to behold, and therefore desperately needs to be addressed. This need coupled with human beings' imaginative ingenuity led us to develop systems of meaning and value that provide frameworks for evaluating ourselves and others as good or bad, successful or otherwise. These systems—*culture*, in a word—do not only comprise morality: they also contain myths that imbue us with cosmic value and even permanence, for ourselves and for the chosen people to which we believe ourselves to belong. Morality and myth almost inevitably come together, so that our individual behaviors take on eternal significance too, being relevant for what happens to us after our mortal lives come to their end. On this account, the need for self-esteem—the need to think well of ourselves, given the cultural values we have imbibed—is a symptom of a much deeper need, a byproduct of the cultural edifices we build to deny death.

It is, as I say, almost too audacious to be true, too grandiose in its ambition. Terror Management Theory is, in effect, a psychological theory of everything. Every human endeavor is supposed to be an *immortality project*: the phrase belongs to Becker himself. The scale of the thing was intoxicating when I first encountered it in undergraduate lectures on social psychology. It is made even more impressive by the large body of experimental evidence—hundreds of published papers—that has accumulated over the decades.[5]

Most of these studies share a simple structure. First, participants are randomly allocated into at least two groups, a *mortality salience* (MS) condition and one or more control conditions. In the MS condition, the participant is reminded of their mortality in some way: most commonly, they are given the writing task at the very beginning of this chapter, asking them to imagine their own dying and death.[6] The control conditions are more variable. In some studies, participants are asked to think and write about a neutral topic like eating or watching television. In others the topic is deliberately more negative, like a painful visit to the dentist or failing an exam. This is to check that not any old unpleasant thoughts will do, only those related to death. After this manipulation, there is usually a *distractor* task, intended to move death from the forefront of participants' minds. Terror Management theorists believe that death thoughts are more powerful when they work unconsciously. Finally, there is some measure of literal or symbolic immortality pursuit.

This can take many forms. Some researchers have asked participants whether they would like to have children, and found that those who thought and wrote about death expressed greater desire for children than those who did not.[7] There is even one study showing that thinking about death increases participants' desire to name their children after themselves![8] Similarly, studies have found that participants in the MS condition were more desirous of fame than those in the control conditions.[9] True to their original interest in self-esteem, studies have also shown that thinking about death motivates us to pursue positive self-esteem.[10] But most Terror Management studies have focused on something they call *worldview defense*: the phenomenon by which we double down on our cultural worldviews when we are confronting our mortality.

Recall that our cultural worldviews provide the value frameworks that allow us to pursue symbolic and literal immortality. They determine the rules of the game that we want to win, if you like. Given that we are committed to winning the game, we must be committed to the game itself. Therefore, according to Terror Management Theory, when we are confronted with our mortality, we are motivated to fight for the validity of our cultural worldviews, whether secular or religious. Often, this comes at the expense of other sources of value. In other words, worldview defense can manifest itself as *prejudice*. Dozens of experiments have found that, relative to those in the control conditions, participants in the MS condition evince more stereotyping, sexism, nationalism, racism, homophobia, and ageism.[11]

Early evidence of religious promiscuity in the face of death

Ken Vail and I were not the first to run experiments on mortality salience and religion. There were, for example, already studies showing that reminders of death increased religious prejudice: Christian prejudice against Jews in particular.[12] Other studies had found that having and affirming religious beliefs can reduce the urge to defend other secular values that participants also hold: if we believe we have literal immortality, we might not need the symbolic variety.[13] And then in 2006, Ara Norenzayan—Will Gervais's doctoral advisor; you might remember from Chapter 2—took things one step further. His paper with Ian Hansen described four experiments and concluded that reminders of death could make us more willing to believe in gods other than our own.

Their fourth experiment is illustrative and fits within the classic Terror Management structure. One hundred forty-two participants were divided into three groups: one MS condition and two different control conditions. In the MS condition, participants completed the standard writing task about death. In one of the control conditions, participants wrote about an experience of dental pain; in the other, they wrote about a more emotionally neutral topic: participation in a team activity. Then, they spent about eight minutes on a distractor task that involved memorizing lists of neutral words like "door" and "sweater."

Finally, came measures of supernatural belief. Participants were given a passage to read, ostensibly a newspaper article from the *South China Morning Post*, which described how the Russian military recruited clairvoyant shamans to help them during and after the Cold War. This is not as far-fetched as it might seem: the Nazis dabbled the most in the occult, but later both the Soviet Union and the United States invested in research into paranormal activity, hoping to weaponize what they discovered. Indeed, the article in this experiment was based on an actual article about the use of clairvoyants by the US military. After reading the passage, participants were asked whether they believed in shamanic spirits and clairvoyance, the effectiveness of the Russian program, and God or a higher power.

This is where it gets a little complicated, and messy. Just over half of the participants were religious—mostly Christian—whereas just under half reported being atheist, agnostic, or otherwise nonreligious. So, Ara and Ian could compare how religious and nonreligious participants responded in their experiment. They found that religious participants were more credulous—even about shamanic spirits—than nonreligious participants. But their initial analyses found no evidence that the MS task made any difference. Crucially, they found no statistical evidence for an *interaction* between the experimental conditions and religiosity, which suggests that the MS task was ineffective for everyone, regardless of religiosity. At this point, researchers are meant to give up: if they dig any deeper, their results should be considered to be unreliable. Ara and Ian did dig deeper. They analyzed the data from the religious and nonreligious participants separately and found that—in contradiction to their initial analysis—the MS task did affect the religious participants but not the nonreligious ones. Religious participants in the MS condition reported higher overall levels of supernatural belief than those in the control conditions. Actually, it is a bit more complicated than that: the MS task increased supernatural belief only when compared to the neutral task but not when compared to the dental pain task. This almost never happens in Terror Management experiments: typically, the MS conditions differs from both control conditions. Unperturbed, they dug deeper still, and found that the increase in supernatural belief was mostly focused on shamanic spirits and clairvoyance. The MS task did not seem to strengthen their belief in God but did push them toward believing in these Siberian ancestral spirits.

Looking back now from the other side of the replication crisis, none of us should have taken this result very seriously. Ara and Ian ran further analyses even when their initial results indicated that they shouldn't have. They then found differences between the MS condition and only one of the control conditions. But the finding was *sexy*. It flew in the face of previous research on worldview defense, and scientists are more easily distracted by contrarian findings than we should be. According to most of the previous research, people defend their own worldviews—religious, secular, or otherwise—in the face of death. And so, we would have expected Ara and Ian's religious participants to report stronger belief in God, and perhaps also decreased belief in shamanic spirits. They found the opposite: the mostly Christian participants became more credulous about shamanic spirits, while their belief in God seemed unaffected. This latter finding—that belief in God was unaffected—not only contradicts other people's previous research, but even one of their own experiments in the same paper. These inconsistencies were red flags, and we should have spotted them.

Regrettably, I looked past these flaws too. All I could think of when I first read the paper was the scene in the 1999 film *The Mummy*, in which a thieving coward Beni Gaboris encounters the eponymous mummy, High Priest Imhotep, freshly resurrected from the dead. Gaboris, terrified out of his wits, first pulls out a Christian cross, attached to a necklace, and begins praying to the Lord to protect him. Noticing that this does not work, he reveals that he is wearing many charms around his neck, and tries them one after another—Muslim, Buddhist, Jewish—in the hope that one of them would dispel Imhotep. (Spoiler: none of them do, but Gaboris survives the encounter.) In a way, Gaboris's actions perfectly rational: if the choice is between literal immortality and a symbolic version, it seems reasonable to opt for the former.

Research, mesearch

We should have tried to replicate this experiment, but we didn't. However, both Ken's and my experiments were variations on the same theme, and therefore very similar to one another. The convergence was entirely accidental, and we had come to these ideas—and to Ara and Ian's paper—from quite different directions. My interest in Terror Management Theory was secondary, as was Ara and Ian's, actually. Instead, my main focus was the evolutionary theories of religion that had been gaining traction since the early 2000s: I was reading books by people like Justin Barrett, Jesse Bering, Pascal Boyer, and Scott Atran, who was Ara Norenzayan's postdoctoral advisor at the University of Michigan. I ended up working on death anxiety, but I could easily have picked any of the other items on my list of factors to begin my work. In contrast, Ken came from a Terror Management stable, under Jamie Arndt at the University of Missouri. Before this, he had worked on political attitudes and attitudes toward war from a Terror Management perspective. Religion is just one slice of the pie for him, as it is for so many people working on Terror Management Theory or in the new field he is helping to build: *existential psychology*. This is not to say that he isn't fascinated by religion in its own right too.

Ken and I also share a personal interest in religion, which is quite rare among the people featured in this book. Of the others, only Justin Barrett would self-identify as religious. Ken's great grandfather on his dad's side was a pastor, and his father is now one too. As a child, Ken went to a Christian school, which held chapel services every morning. Far from rebelling against it at the time, he took it all very seriously, and was amazed that others didn't: after all, spiritual matters mattered, they had eternal significance. From a young age, he was convinced he should dedicate himself entirely to spiritual development, and even leadership. He was headed, like his great grandfather, to the seminary and the church.

His plans to take up the cloth were waylaid, at first by the Olympic Training Center in Colorado Springs, who had invited him to be a resident athlete there. Shooting was his sport.

"Trap and skeet," he elaborated, which I then had to look up, and would probably still misdescribe. I observed to him that he picked guns over Jesus, and he responded by pointing out that God and guns go together in many parts of the United States. Besides, the US Olympic Committee offered him free room and board, training including a sports psychologist, and free college at the nearby University of Colorado in Colorado Springs. So off he went. They even suggested that he take up psychology as his major, under the mistaken assumption that it would be beneficial for his shooting performance: it's a head game, after all, they figured. This too is more reasonable than Bruce Hood's idea that psychology might teach him to be Uri Gellar.

It was Mollie Maxfield who introduced Ken to Terror Management Theory. She was Tom Pyszczynski's graduate student and happened to be teaching the social psychology class that he was inevitably late for, having had to dash from shooting training just before. His sports psychologist suggested that he volunteer as a research assistant for her, to curry favor and to cure his boredom. By this point in his life—his third year in college—he had already left the spectacularly American "god and guns" culture behind, which is not quite the same thing as leaving either God or guns behind. But as he puts it, the threads to the sweater were beginning to unravel religion-wise, partly from bad experiences in his Roman Catholic high school, partly from his frustrations over American Christian support for George W. Bush's war in Iraq, and partly from what he was learning in classes about comparative religion and history of religion. All the same, he still felt the pull toward faith.

Terror Management Theory gave Ken a way out for good. It helped him make sense of this pull he felt, as well as of the eagerness of his country to wage war to defend and propagate its values. According to the theory, these were both the psychological products of his own death anxiety.

"Research is *me*search," he says to me, and I understand entirely. My relationship with faith and science is very different from Ken's, but like him, I saw how Terror Management Theory could help me understand myself, including my own pull toward religious faith. He's not wrong about research being mesearch.

Foxhole atheism

Both of our experiments were modifications of Ara Norenzayan and Ian Hansen's original. Ken's compared Christians and *atheists*, just over two dozen of each, all psychology undergraduates at the University of Missouri–Columbia. My participants were undergraduates at the University of Otago, about 50 Christians and about 50 nonreligious folk, people who said that they were atheists, agnostics, or had no religious affiliation. This difference in our samples might have turned out to be important, as we shall see. In both our experiments, as with Ara and Ian's, participants were assigned to the MS writing task or a control condition. In Ken's case, the control condition asked participants to think and write about experiencing "something turning out differently than you had expected." In mine, it asked them to think and write about watching television. There's no reason to think that this difference in control conditions mattered: they rarely do in Terror Management research. What might have done is the fact that Ken followed standard Terror Management theory protocol and included a distractor task—a short questionnaire about the participants' mood and a word search task—whereas I did not, for reasons we will get to later.

Our measures differed too, reflecting our particular research interests. I wanted to know if people—religious and nonreligious—would be more likely to entertain supernatural beliefs in general when they were confronted with thoughts about their mortality. In other words, I wanted to test the old adage about there being no atheists in foxholes, if by "foxhole" we mean soundproof and dark cubicles purpose-built for our lab. To do this, my colleagues and I constructed a questionnaire, which we called the *Supernatural Belief Scale* (SBS). The SBS asks participants how much they agree with 10 statements about the existence of God, angels, demons, heaven, hell, miracles, prophecies, and so forth. As with most scales, participants' responses to the 10 items of the SBS are then averaged together to form a single score: this indicates a person's willingness to believe in supernatural entities and events in general, without focusing on any particular thing.

Ken's interests were more along the lines of the Ben Gaboris scene, and therefore closer to Ara and Ian's study: he wanted to know whether people would become religiously promiscuous when they thought about death. He adapted measures from one of Ara and Ian's other experiments in the same paper, asking participants about the "Buddha," "Allah," and "God (Jesus)."[14] In each case, participants were asked about how much they agreed or disagreed—on a scale of 1 to 10, with 10 indicating strong agreement—that the deity in question exists, answers prayers, and intervenes in worldly matters.

Unhelpfully, our results—Ken's, mine, and Ara and Ian's—were inconsistent. If we had all found more-or-less the same things, we could count our experiments as convergent evidence: conceptual replications of the same phenomenon. Had Ken and I attempted to directly replicate Ara and Ian's work, we might have been able to determine whether the earlier experimental results were wrong. As it was, we were left with the job of trying to figure out *why* our results disagreed. Let's take each of the three main findings in turn.

The first question we tried to answer was whether religious people bolster their beliefs when they are reminded about death. On this front, our results were quite consistent with one another. Ken's participants reported stronger belief in "God (Jesus)" when they were made to think about death; mine had higher SBS scores under the same conditions. Ara and Ian also found a similar effect in some of their experiments, though notably not in the one described above. So, there wasn't *perfect* agreement, but this wasn't half bad. Unfortunately, it was downhill from there.

The second question that the other two studies tried to answer, but not mine, was whether or not religious people are religiously *promiscuous* when they are confronted with their mortality. Ara and Ian's mostly Christian participants showed less skepticism about shamanic spirits in the MS condition than in the control condition. Ken found no hint of this when his Christian participants were asked about Allah or the Buddha: on the contrary, they expressed stronger *dis*belief in these foreign gods under MS. On this question, they have perfect disagreement.

Finally, all three of our experiments looked at how nonreligious participants would respond in the MS condition. This time, my experiment was the outlier: my nonreligious participants reported greater religious disbelief in the MS condition than in the control condition. This is arguably what Terror Management Theory would lead us to expect: nonreligious people defending their secular worldview in the face of death. However, neither of the other two studies found any such effect.

I am still not entirely sure how to account for the differences between these findings. One possibility is that some of the findings were flukes, Ara and Ian's result on religious promiscuity and mine on foxhole atheism in particular. For one thing, the effects were quite small. Recall that Ara and Ian's initial analyses found no effects, which made their further analyses improper. Having runs further analyses, their findings were at risk of being the result of false positive errors. In my case, the nonreligious participants scored less than one point higher out of a maximum score of nine on the SBS in the MS condition than in the control condition. In other words, these findings might not replicate. This is the most straightforward explanation, but there are others worth considering.

For example, Ken ran his study in the American South,[15] whereas Ara and Ian ran theirs in Canada. It is not implausible that Christians are more fervent in their beliefs in Missouri than in Vancouver, and therefore less malleable toward belief in shamanic spirits. Furthermore, Ken's *nonreligious* sample consisted exclusively of *atheists*, whereas self-described atheists only made up about 10% of my sample: most of my nonreligious sample were just people who did not identify with any organized religion. It is not implausible that atheists' religious disbeliefs are firmer than other nonbelievers', less amenable to modification by any experimental manipulation. Unfortunately, Ara and Ian did not specify how atheistic their nonreligious sample was, but if this explanation is right, then their sample should look more like Ken's than like mine.

A third possibility is that the distractor task between the MS task and the supernatural belief questions made a difference: Ken's and Ara and Ian's both included it, whereas mine did not. When my paper was sent out by journal editors for peer review, several of the reviewers mentioned the lack of a distractor task as an unwelcome deviation from the norm established in research on Terror Management Theory. But it was omitted for a reason. According to the theory, the job of the distractor task is to stop participants from consciously attending to their death thoughts: the idea is that the thoughts themselves are still there, lurking just beneath the surface, but that participants are unaware of it. It is when death thoughts are unconscious that they are meant to trigger the interesting effects repeatedly reported by Terror Management Theorists. There is, however, a caveat to this: unconscious death thoughts trigger *distal* responses whereas conscious death thoughts trigger *proximal* ones. According to an elaboration of the theory in the 1990s,[16] proximal responses are those that deal directly with the threat of death, for example by intending to exercise more or engage in other health-promoting behaviors;[17] distal responses are those that involve enhancing one's self-esteem or defending one's cultural worldview, as typically found in studies of Terror Management Theory. I considered supernatural belief—which, after all, included belief in an afterlife—to be a proximal response, one that directly addresses the problem of mortality by positing literal immortality. If I am right about this, then increased supernatural belief—or, more appropriately, reduced skepticism—might be a proximal rather than a distal response to death thoughts, which would explain why we do find this effect when there is no distractor task and don't when there is.

Ken and I have discussed trying to adjudicate between these possibilities, but—seven years after our papers were first published—we have not done so yet. Science is a process, and sometimes progress is slow. The next step is actually fairly obvious. We should first agree on our control conditions and our religiosity measures, and then recruit a very large sample. The rule-of-thumb for replications is to at least double the number of participants of the original study. It would also be good to deliberately sample atheists, as Ken did, so we can analyze their results separately from more vaguely nonreligious folk. We should then run a version of the study with and one without the distractor task, to see if that makes a difference. This is what we—or someone else—should do, but I don't know when it will actually happen.

Death and implicit religiosity

Ken's and my papers contained three studies each, the first of which we have just seen. After that, we moved in quite different directions. Ken got in touch with an Iranian collaborator—Abdolhossein Abdollahi, now at the University of Texas in El Paso—and they repeated the first study among Iranian Muslims, replicating their initial results with Christians. Muslims who were reminded of their mortality believed more in Allah but less in the Buddha and "God (Jesus)."[18] Admittedly, there is something odd about asking Muslims whether they believe "God (Jesus) exists" because they don't equate God with Jesus, but Ken and his team wanted to maintain consistency across studies. His third study returned to the United States and turned the spotlight onto people who described themselves as agnostics,[19] and this time the nonreligious participants reported *higher* levels of religiosity, belief in a higher power, and belief in Allah, the Buddha, and God (Jesus) when confronted with their mortality. In other words, they behaved the opposite of the nonreligious participants in my study, who reported strong *dis*belief after they thought about death. The discrepancy grows.[20]

Rather than pivoting to different samples, I turned to a different method of measuring supernatural beliefs. The most common way of measuring someone's beliefs, supernatural or otherwise, is to ask them. But, as we have already seen in previous chapters, psychologists often want to avoid asking people direct questions. Sometimes, as in the case of experiments on infants, this is because there is a language barrier. Sometimes, as in the case of Justin Barrett's experiment, this is because psychologists want to see if there is anything else going on underneath our orthodoxies. This has also been a concern among social psychologists for the better part of the last decade. Within social psychology, *indirect measures* came about mostly to see whether people still held racist attitudes even though they would claim to disavow such views.

As I alluded to in the introductory chapter, the body of research on indirect measures of attitudes has enjoyed some publicity recently, as interest in implicit bias has grown. Implicit biases are prejudices—say against people of different ethnicities, genders, or sexual orientations—that exist within us and affect our behavior even if we are not aware of them. Implicit racial prejudice has been blamed for police violence against Black Americans, for example; implicit sexism is widely seen as the cause of injustices in hiring and other workplace practices. Some people believe that we can measure such implicit biases by using certain indirect measures. These types of tasks are sometimes called *implicit measures*, but this term is contested. Indeed, the whole idea of implicit attitudes, including implicit biases, is controversial among cognitive psychologists. Not everyone believes they even exist.

While I was a graduate student, my advisor Jamin Halberstadt had a visiting postdoctoral researcher who had just spent a few years working with the Implicit Association Test at the University of Heidelberg. The IAT is— like the concept of implicit biases itself—not without its controversies. Some people think that it measures implicit biases; others think that it measures our knowledge of culturally prevalent beliefs and attitudes that we might not ourselves hold; still others think it measures a bit of both those things or something in between. Before he came to us, Matthias Bluemke had spent the previous five or six years trying to figure out whether and how the IAT works. With some cajoling, Matthias agreed to help me to design an IAT to measure supernatural beliefs. I only discovered later on that Ara had beat me to it a few years earlier, though he had not applied it to Terror Management experiments.[21] In fact, no one had.

The IAT is a reaction time task, like the ones designed by Adam Cohen and Ben Purzycki discussed two chapters ago. In those cases, participants respond to a single task with two options: real or imaginary, yes or no. IATs are a bit more complex in that they involve *two* tasks at the same time, often two different categorization tasks. Our IAT had only had one categorization task and one simpler reaction time task. The categorization task required participants to classify synonyms for *real* and *imaginary* respectively. So, if they saw words like "genuine" or "actual" they would press one key, and if they saw words like "fake" or "illusory" they would press another. The other task simply required participants to press a key whenever they saw words referring to supernatural things like god, hell, and spirit. Where it gets less simple is that in one phase of the task, the key they had to press for the *supernatural* words was the same one as for *real* words; and in another phase, they had to press the same key as the *imaginary* words. This allows us to compute a score that compares how quickly participants respond to the supernatural words in the two different phases. The relative speeds basically tell us how easy or difficult participants find each pairing. Believers should react faster when supernatural and real are paired to the same key, whereas nonbelievers should react faster when supernatural and imaginary are paired. And they do: IAT scores are positively, albeit only mildly, correlated with scores on self-report measures of religiosity.[22]

The experiment we ran with our new IAT was structurally identical to the previous one with the Supernatural Belief Scale. We recruited 42 Christians and 59 nonreligious participants, psychology undergraduates from the University of Otago, and had them do either the MS or the watching TV writing task. This was followed immediately by the IAT, again without a distractor task. We found that the Christian participants had on average higher IAT scores than the nonreligious participants, which was unsurprising. We also found that—regardless of whether they were Christian or nonreligious—participants in the MS condition had higher IAT scores than those in the control condition. In other words, writing about death *increased* supernatural belief for both religious and nonreligious people.

This result contradicts the earlier experiment with the Supernatural Belief Scale, in which nonreligious participants showed classic worldview defense effects: in that study, they were *more* skeptical of supernaturalia in the MS condition than in the control condition. Here, they were *less* skeptical in the

MS than in the control condition. This suggests that nonreligious folk are, in some sense, tempted toward faith when they are confronted with their mortality. But if you have gained anything from this book so far, it is surely not to take any single study's results for granted. All the experiments described in this chapter require replication, but perhaps this one most of all, given how controversial the IAT is.

"In some sense" is a weasel's way of saying that I don't really know what's going on, and indeed I don't. Even assuming that IAT scores are meaningful and that this experimental result is robust and replicable, it is still not straightforward to interpret. A lot turns on what one makes of IATs and their scores. Are we saying, for example, that when reminded about death nonreligious people *deceptively* report increased disbelief but really, deep down inside, question their religious skepticism? Or are we saying that they are of two minds, trenchant in their atheism at one level but tempted toward belief at another? From our data alone, we can really say none of these things for sure.

A long way to go

This book began with a defense of sorts of the possibility of experimental psychology, even for something like religion. In principle, the experimental method in psychology is not so very different from the experimental method in medicine or chemistry or physics. The logic of manipulating conditions and measuring outcomes to infer causation is constant across disciplines. But the devil is in the details, and we have seen that the details of psychological research can be devilish. For starters, chemists and physicists have much more control than we do in psychology, and even in medicine: human beings vary more from individual to individual than do protons or vials of hydrocyanic acid. Psychologists have to reckon with cultural differences as well as individual ones: American humans might respond differently in our experiments than Tuvan humans; adult humans differently from younger humans; Christian humans from Buddhist humans from the varieties of nonreligious humans.

Which brings us back to difficulties of measurement, also more straightforward in the physical sciences, even though it too is often indirect. The IAT is not the only measure in my study that deserves scrutiny. Every experiment discussed in this chapter divided participants into categories: religious

v. nonreligious, agnostic, and atheist. These too are acts of measurement, which is just the practical instantiation of definition. As we can see from these studies, methods of categorization are negotiable, and our findings may well depend on the choices we make. In every one of the studies in this chapter, we relied on how participants labeled themselves to categorize them. But identity labels can tell us only so much about a person, and it is not always clear what they do tell us.

We may call ourselves "Christian" because we believe the contents of the ecumenical creeds or because we faithfully attend mass on Easter and Christmas or because we consider Christian self-identification as a sign of patriotism, whether English, American, or Russian. We may claim our religion as "none" because we disagree that "atheist" is a religious affiliation, though we reject all supernatural belief: or perhaps we just don't like the label "atheist" because it carries with it the baggage of immorality or communism. There is no easy answer to the question of how best to divide people into groups based on their characteristics because social and psychological categories are not *natural kinds*. We know exactly what a proton is and what hydrocyanic acid is: there are watertight definitions of these. Not so for objects in psychology, or even in biology. This explains why there is diversity in how different scientists choose to categorize people: there are no firm objective criteria to adjudicate between definitions.

And even if we had measurement sorted out, there is the challenge of experimental manipulation. Psychologists don't always know what they are manipulating. Often, our manipulations only approximate the causal factors we are really interested in, for practical and ethical reasons. Consider, for example, the question of whether analytic thinking promotes atheism. The ideal experiment would be to take two groups of babies, and train one of them to think analytically: the two groups should differ in no other way than this. And then, many years later, we could observe to see whether the babies trained to think analytically were more likely to be atheists than the other babies. This is not a feasible experiment to run, which leaves us with correlational and longitudinal research, and lab experiments like Will Gervais's studies. The Rodin manipulation is a proxy for an upbringing that emphasizes analytic thinking. The MS task is a proxy for poignant moments and scary ones, when we are confronted with the inevitability of our mortality: the death of a loved one, a terminal diagnosis, a terrorist attack.

The trouble is that the MS task—designed to test *Terror* Management Theory—is not at all terrifying: studies have consistently found that it is not a very scary task.[23] It might work better to trick people into thinking that they are at heightened risk of a life-threatening disease or that their life expectancy is unusually short. Psychologists are not beneath this kind of deception, but our ethics review boards might have concerns. Even more effectively—and ethically dubious—we could generate the acute feeling of mortal peril, as the neuroscientist David Eagleman has done. He once had participants fall 150 feet, upside down, without any sort of harness, into a net.[24] That study was about our experience of time, and you should definitely look it up. The point is that the MS task is nothing like these, and therefore cannot really be said to tell us anything directly about whether death *anxiety* motivates religious belief. The most we will be able to say is that death *thoughts* might temporarily affect our religious beliefs in some way, which is not quite the same thing. Perhaps as a result of its methodology, Terror Management Theory is now mostly a theory about death thoughts rather than a theory about the fear of death.

All of which is to say that these studies that Ken and I ran in graduate school are suggestive starting points, nothing more but certainly nothing less. They need to be replicated—both directly and conceptually—and improved on in various ways. This is true, in a sense, of all the experiments we have looked at. Will Gervais's experiment may have failed to replicate, but analytic thinking does seem to be correlated with supernatural belief: perhaps a future experiment will tell us whether and how this relationship is causal. Deb Kelemen's work certainly suggests that children think of natural things as if they were artifacts: it is still not clear whether this has much to do with *religion* as we commonly think of it. It is easy to see the flaws and limitations in Justin Barrett's vignettes and Cristine Legare's simpatias, but the hard work of improving on them has yet to be done. Bruce Hood's dualism experiment and Ben Purzycki's study on what gods know—and, indeed, all these experiments—still need to be run in other cultures to see exactly how widespread these biases are. Some of this follow-up work is indeed being done, and we shall see the fruits of this labor soon.

Psychologists have been interested in religion since the very beginning of the discipline. Wilhelm Wundt, William James, Sigmund Freud, and other luminaries of the early history of the field, were all fascinated by religion, and had their hypotheses about why people are religious. *Experimental* psychological research on religion is relatively new: developmental and cross-cultural experimental research even more so. We still have a long way to go, a lot of work to do, conceptually, methodologically, and empirically. There are still many controversies to resolve, about definition, measurement, and manipulation. There are even controversies about what phenomena exist at all to be studied: we do not yet know if there is such a thing as *implicit religiosity*, for example. But ignorance and confusion is where science often begins. Indeed, this is where many exciting sciences have begun, from the study of bacteria to the study of black holes, the existences of which were long under doubt before they were taken for granted. Of course, it might all come to naught, but there is only one way to find out.

Epilogue

In the preceding pages, I have tried to tell stories about experiments, and about the people who thought them up and conducted them to discover something about how our minds work. In writing this book, I had hoped for two outcomes, one more for the reader and the other more for myself. My hope for the reader was and is that you will gain some appreciation of how experimental psychologists think, how we make decisions about the questions we ask, the contexts in which we ask them, and the methods we employ to eke out answers, which are so often uncertain, even fickle.

Psychology is a difficult science, which our forebears knew: the first generation of experimental psychologists in the 19th century focused almost exclusively on basic cognitive and perceptual phenomena. They ran experiments about how many numbers we can remember at any given time, and how we tell very similar colors and sounds apart. Wilhelm Wundt himself, often credited as the founder of experimental psychology, argued that the experimental methods he pioneered had their limitations, and that religion fell well beyond them. His own researches about religion look to modern eyes more like comparative history and anthropology than like experimental psychology.

This brings us to my second hope, which was to gain a better sense for myself whether Wundt was right, after all, to be skeptical about this kind of experimenting with religion, and indeed with any complex human psychological phenomena. This book began during a crisis of faith: not in God or the Church, but in experimental psychology as a scientific enterprise. The replication crisis—described in Chapter 2—shook many of us who were just at the start of our careers at the time. We could no longer trust any of the classic experimental results in our textbooks, or even those we built on in our own research. Indeed, our own work was now questionable; perhaps even our new skills as experimentalists were worth less than we thought.

Experimenting with Religion. Jonathan Jong, Oxford University Press. © Oxford University Press 2023.
DOI: 10.1093/oso/9780190875541.003.0009

Even now, people are trying to diagnose the problems in psychological science, en route to figuring out what we can do to improve matters. Some people emphasize the importance of more rigorous training in statistics; others insist that incentive structures in academia are toxic, and need to be changed to encourage better—and slower—science; others still predict that our methodological problems will remain until our theories become more formal and perhaps more mathematical. These are all plausible suggestions, but the arguments can be quite abstract: I hoped that this reconsideration of particular studies would help clarify things for me, and perhaps even point a way forward.

As the replication crisis itself reminds us, it is a dangerous thing to draw conclusions from a small handful of cases. The set of studies we have encountered in this book is by no means exhaustive, but experimenting with religion turns out to be much less common than you might think. In 1977, the legendary social psychologist C. Daniel Batson could only think of *one* experiment on religion: the Marsh Chapel Experiment briefly described in Chapter 1.[1] Things have improved somewhat, but the sample of experiments in which some aspect of religiosity is measured is still very small. My conclusions are therefore necessarily tentative.

Between- v. within-subjects experiments

As I was reading through these studies—and subsequent attempts to replicate them—it occurred to me that experiments with a *between-subjects* design fared poorly compared to those with a *within-subjects* design. Recall from Chapter 1 that a between-subjects experiment is one that compares between individuals or groups, whereas a within-subjects experiment is one that looks within individuals or groups, such as in a before-and-after comparison. Bruce Hood's, Jesse Bering's, and most of Deb Kelemen's experiments were within-subject experiments, and their findings have survived replication attempts, albeit rarely exact or direct replications. In contrast, many between-subjects experiments on religion have failed to replicate. Most conspicuously, Will Gervais's study with *The Thinker* was a between-subjects experiment, as was Amitai Shenav's study on the same theme, as were the experiments on death anxiety we have just encountered in Chapter 8. The former two decisively failed to replicate, and the latter have produced rather unreliable results: indeed, other experiments using the same methods from

Terror Management Theory have also failed to replicate.[2] There are at least two more examples of between-subjects experiments not covered in this book that have either failed to replicate or are unlikely to do so.

The more amusing of the two was by a team from the University of Chicago and Harvard.[3] In this study, people are given a personality quiz, a bit more realistic than the ones on *Buzzfeed*. At the end of the quiz, participants are told that their test results are actually pretty good predictors of certain future outcomes. Half the participants are then told that—based on their quiz results—they are quite likely to live ordinary happy lives, surrounded by friends and family. The other half are told that they will probably end up alone forever. This was to make them feel lonely, though I imagine it would have also made me feel sad. In any case, when asked later whether they believed in God, the Devil, ghosts, and other such things, the participants who were made to feel lonely reported higher levels of belief than those who were not. I know of no attempt to replicate this study, but the original version was statistically *underpowered*: its sample was much smaller than it should have been given the small size of the effect they found. It is possible that an attempt to replicate the finding with a 50% larger sample—the minimum required—would succeed: but I doubt it.

The one that has already failed to replicate involved asking participants to recall and write about a positive event, one that made them feel happy or can otherwise be characterized as having a good outcome.[4] This is probably more pleasant than imagining and writing about one's own death, but it is the same kind of task. The experimental manipulation was in the details of the instructions. For half the participants, the instructions specified that the event had to be one that they had *absolutely no* control over: perhaps it was a matter of good luck or the kindness of a stranger. For the other half, the instructions specified the event had to be one that they had *total* control over: perhaps a wise decision or an achievement won with hard work. In other words, some participants were made to feel less in control of the world while others were made to feel more in control of the world, or so that's what the experimenters intend. After this writing task, participants were asked whether they believed that events in the world were at least partly controlled by God, or something like God, in accordance with a plan. In the original study, participants who recalled an event in which they had no control reported higher levels of belief in a God who has a plan and is in control: the researchers concluded that belief in such a God compensates for the perceived lack of control. This is, like many of the other between-subjects studies, a neat experiment, almost beautifully simple in its logic and execution. But it doesn't replicate. The team that ran the replication, which included one of the authors of the original experiment, calculated that the original sample was about 10 times smaller than it needed to be: when they re-ran the experiment with a more appropriate sample size, they found no effect.[5]

I would be remiss if I did not mention that the Marsh Chapel experiment is also a between-subjects experiment. Recall that the seminarians who received psilocybin before a two-and-a-half hour long Good Friday service were much more likely to have meaningful mystical experiences than those who received a placebo. They felt one with the world and in awe of it; they felt like they had gained some unspeakable insight about reality; they felt joy and peace and love. But—and this is rarely mentioned in descriptions of the study—they did not feel more deeply that God loved them; nor did they feel closer to God, compared to their sober fellow seminarians. To the extent that religion is primarily about gods, the Marsh Chapel experiment produced mystical experiences without affecting religiosity per se.

Are religious beliefs manipulable?

I confess I don't know why between-subjects experiments are so unpromising, but there are a few possibilities to consider. The most pessimistic possibility is that religious beliefs are simply not amenable to change by experimental manipulation. The logic of between-subjects experiments assumes that such change is possible, but perhaps this assumption is misguided in our case. After all, religious beliefs are often held with some conviction, together with other beliefs that are important parts of our identities.

Within-subjects experiments can be used to study such changes too, of course: indeed, it seems the more obvious method to do so, as talk of change typically implies before-and-after comparisons of the same individuals. Between-subjects experiments might reveal differences between conditions, which we attribute to the experimental manipulation. The inference that the manipulation—say, the reminders of death or the images of *The Thinker* or the prediction of future loneliness—affected the individuals in question is one step removed from what is actually observed. And yet, despite the relative appropriateness of within-subjects experiments for studying changes in belief, those we have encountered have not examined such changes and do not, in fact, take the form of before-and-after comparisons.

Psychologists are generally reluctant to run before-and-after experiments because we worry about asking participants the same questions twice. Participants sometimes guess the intent of the experiment when we do this, which might affect their behavior in unpredictable ways that skew our data, so we avoid this before-and-after setup. Perhaps it is simply easier to reveal stable intuitions and other deep-seated psychological tendencies relevant to religion than it is to change beliefs in measurable ways.

I don't know if religious beliefs are impervious to experimental manipulation, but I do have some sense of how difficult the job might be. Not long after I finished graduate school, my advisor Jamin Halberstadt and I worked with a postdoctoral researcher—and standup comedian—Brittany Cardwell on over a dozen experiments, all attempting to shift people's religious beliefs. Brittany came up with all kinds of ideas, applying tried-and-true techniques from the psychological literature on persuasion to this task. My favorite manipulation relied on something called the "use of retrieval" effect.[6]

The basic theory here is that the ease with which information is recalled affects our beliefs, even about ourselves. This might be why so many people are afraid of flying, despite the very low risk of dying in a plane crash; because plane crashes are so intensely publicized, it is quite easy to think of examples like the recent Malaysian Airlines MH370 and MH17 cases, not to mention the incidents of September 11, 2001.

In their seminal study, Norbert Schwarz and his colleagues manipulated ease of retrieval by asking people to recall either six or 12 occasions during which they behaved assertively. They found that those asked to recall six occasions—easier to do than recalling 12, except perhaps for the hyperassertive—gave themselves higher assertiveness ratings. Over 200 studies have since been published on this effect, using variations of this basic methodology. Across more studies than we can now remember, we asked participants to provide either three or 12 reasons for believing or disbelieving in God, hoping to find that this would affect their beliefs. It didn't: or rather, it did sometimes, which is to say that the effects were not robust to replication.

In total, Brittany thinks we ran over a hundred studies, using different techniques. Some studies included biased questionnaires full of leading questions that would subtly force participants to respond as if they were religious; we thought that responding religiously might actually make people feel more religious, at least temporarily. Other studies involved fabricated newspaper articles or even scientific journal articles that somehow supported religious beliefs or indicated some benefits to being religious. Others still had participants thinking and writing about things that they thought science could not explain: the idea here was that the explanatory gap might nudge people toward believing in supernatural causes. Nothing we tried worked well or reliably enough to be considered a success.

Now, it is possible that we failed time and time again just because people are intransigent about their religious beliefs. But it is also possible that our manipulations were not the right ones; or perhaps they were too weak; or perhaps our measurement instruments were insufficiently sensitive to detect subtle and transient fluctuations in belief. These possibilities all apply to the other between-subjects experiments we have discussed as well.

There are reasons to push back against this most pessimistic take on things. For starters, although religious beliefs are sometimes held with great conviction, this is hardly always the case. It is quite easy to see from survey data that people are neither staunch atheists nor dogmatic theists: a lot of people are somewhere in between, their beliefs held with less certainty and therefore potentially more lightly. Furthermore, even if our articulated religious positions are stable, we might still experience fleeting doubts or surges of piety. Finally, Deb Kelemen's work on speeded and unspeeded tasks provides one example of a between-subjects experiment that seems robust, even across cultures: even if we are unable to shift participants' beliefs, perhaps we can study different conditions under which their intuitions are more-or-less concealed.

The example of Deb's work makes me think that our methods of measurement are not up to the job of detecting the kinds of changes—likely to be subtle and fleeting—that result from experimental manipulations. It is a poor worker who blames his tools, but we need not dwell in poverty. If this diagnosis of the situation is correct, then the solution is to develop and use more sensitive measures than traditional questionnaires. We have encountered a few candidates already, besides Deb's speeded task: Justin Barrett looked at biases in memory, and Ben Purzycki and I measured reaction times, for example. The trouble with these kinds of techniques is that they are more difficult to interpret than straightforward self-report measures. Unlike the case of self-report measures of religiosity, there are practically no implicit measures of religiosity that have been subjected to rigorous checks for reliability and validity. Fortunately, this is a fixable problem.

Psychological states v. traits

Questions about whether our manipulations are the right ones or whether they are sufficiently powerful are more difficult to answer and reveal a fundamental limitation of experimental psychological research as practiced here. The problem is not just that our manipulations in the laboratory are watered-down versions of experiences in real life, as we have seen in the difference between the standard mortality salience manipulation in Terror Management experiments and a bona fide threat to one's life. There is a broader issue, which is that the vast majority of psychology experiments—and not just those about religion—are designed to study psychological states rather than psychological traits.

The distinction between psychological traits and states is an important one, not least because it is unclear how they are related to one another. There are ongoing debates, for example, about whether one's dispositional happiness is simply a sum of how frequently one experiences happy feelings or whether there is more to it than this, maybe a happy disposition can actually contribute to experiences of happiness. Analogous questions arise about the relationship between a person's religiosity and their moments of doubt or conviction.

This inferential gap between psychological traits and states generates one between our experiments and the questions we have about the real world, which tend to be about religiosity as a trait. We want to know why some people are religious while others aren't, and indeed why religion is a stable and recurring feature across cultures. So, even if we discovered that, say, reminders of death reliably nudge people toward religious belief, it is not obvious what this would tell us about the role that thoughts and feelings about death play in religion in the real world.

Correlational and longitudinal studies

This is where other methods in the psychologist's toolkit come in. Correlational studies—like Francis Galton's study of prayer and longevity mentioned in the first chapter of this book—can contribute converging evidence, though correlational data are difficult to interpret in causal terms. The religiosity–death anxiety link actually provides a neat example of the problem. What correlational pattern would we expect if the fear of death were an important motivation toward religious belief? On one hand, we might expect people who have a more intense fear of death to find religious beliefs more attractive. On the other, if religious beliefs are actually comforting, then we might expect devoutly religious folk to be less anxious about death. Perhaps we can combine these two insights and predict a positive correlation between these two traits among nonbelievers and a negative correlation among believers. As it turns out, however, if there is any correlation at all—positive, negative, or both—between death anxiety and religious belief, it is weak and varies from country to country. We might take this as an indication that death anxiety plays a minor role at best in motivating religious belief in the real world, regardless of what we manage to find in the lab.

There is one further tool psychologists can use, but it is expensive and labor intensive. I mentioned longitudinal studies in Chapter 3. Deb wanted to know whether the children who rejected teleological explanations would be more likely to grow up to be atheists: to find out, she would have to track down those children—now adults—and ask them about their religious beliefs. Better still if she had tracked these children as they grew up, to see how their relationships to religion evolved over time. That way, she would be able to statistically control for inevitable variations in life experiences.

This kind of longitudinal study that follows individuals from childhood to adulthood is not unheard of in psychology, but it is rare and none—as far as I know—focus on religion. On the bright side, several large-scale, long-term projects do include measures of religiosity, so we can glean *something* from them. In the United Kingdom, the most exciting of these is the Avon Longitudinal Study of Parents and Children (ALSPAC) that began in the early 1990s with around 15,000 newborns and their parents. As is common in many longitudinal studies—and especially one as demanding as the ALSPAC—many participants have since dropped out or been lost to death, but there are still nearly six thousand active participants. The dataset—still growing—includes all kind of information about the physical and mental health of parents and children, as well as genetic data and IQ data: there is even information about the parents' religiosity, taken at three time points: just before the birth of the child, five years after, and nine years after. The children are now adults, and this wealth of data provides the opportunity for testing hypotheses about which children grow up to be religious or irreligious or somewhere in between.[7]

Longitudinal studies are not experiments and cannot test causal hypotheses in quite the same way. But statistical controls can make up for the lack of experimental control to some extent, assuming that we have the relevant information at the relevant time points. In the case of ALSPAC, for example, we can look at whether childhood IQ predicts adult religiosity controlling for things like parental religiosity during the child's upbringing, the child's educational attainment, and other variables whose effects we want to rule out. This would provide better evidence than Miron Zuckerman's analysis of correlational data, mentioned briefly in Chapter 2. His dataset comprised IQ and religiosity data taken at the same time in adulthood: it therefore cannot tell us which one came first, the intelligence or the religiosity.

The fact that the ALSPAC was not designed to study people's religious beliefs does limit the kinds of questions we can ask of its data, of course. Indeed, almost none of the hypotheses we focused on in this book are directly testable using ALSPAC data, which did not collect data on teleological intuitions or anthropomorphic ones, or those related to dualism or analytic thinking. The exception to this is the one about mortality salience and religiosity: the ALSPAC data might be able to tell us whether life-threatening illnesses or experiences predict subsequences changes in religious belief.

The ALSPAC is not the only longitudinal study around amenable to psychologists who are interested in religion, though it might be the largest. Out of allegiance to and nostalgia for New Zealand, I should mention at least two projects based there. The Dunedin Multidisciplinary Health and Development Study is rather like the ALSPAC, but on a much smaller scale: it started with over a thousand newborns—almost every child born between April 1972 and 1973—and has followed them ever since, with remarkably few people dropping out, under 10%, after all this time. Religiosity data has only been collected twice so far, when the participants were 26 and 32 years old, respectively, but even this is enough to test various hypotheses.[8]

The New Zealand Attitudes and Values Study (NZAVS), which started in 2009 and was initially planned to last 20 years, takes a rather different form. Rather than following a single cohort over decades, the NZAVS adds new people every year, while keeping around 80% of the participants from the previous year: this annual attrition rate means that fewer than half of the original 6,500 or so participants have remained in the study, but because of new recruits every year, the current sample is twice the size of the original and the total number of participants is now well over 30,000. The NZAVS is particularly interesting for our purposes because it includes more religiosity measures than the ALSPAC and Dunedin Study, which has already resulted in quite a few important studies on religiosity, including one—speaking of life-threatening events—about how the major earthquakes in Christchurch in 2011 affected people's religious identities.[9]

All of which is to say that psychological research on religion neither begins nor ends with experiments. Experiments allow us to peer under the hoods of our minds to see in action the intuitions that undergird our articulated beliefs. They might even be able to show us how and why our beliefs fluctuate under different circumstances. But this information is only part of the story about why so many people believe in gods, souls, and rituals, and why some don't. Of course, even with our whole gamut of methods, psychologists can only address a part of the question. Other social scientists—sociologists, anthropologists, economists, and historians in particular—will have their part to play in helping us understand this most curious and compelling aspect of being human.

Experimental anthropology

For the most part, I will have to leave the task of describing the work of other social scientists to someone else. However, psychologists have already begun to engage in interdisciplinary work, and one such approach is worth mentioning here. We already have an example of it in Ben Purzycki's work, which combines ethnographic research typical among anthropologists with experimental psychological methods. This is sometimes called *experimental anthropology*, and it is gaining ground in the social scientific study of religion.

Experimental anthropology is a bold attempt to exceed the limitations of traditional ethnography on one hand and laboratory-based experimental psychology on the other, while retaining both their strengths. Since the early decades of the 20th century, anthropologists have generally shied away from making broad and general claims about human beings: instead, they have focused on studying particular human phenomena in particular cultures. At the risk of caricature, the modus operandi of an anthropologist is to move to a foreign country, and live there for months or even years, observing the details of certain cultural practices and interviewing their practitioners. What results is typically a rich description and interpretation of these specific practices in their social and historical contexts, with very little by way of extrapolation or generalization.

This shift toward *particularism* was a reaction to what anthropologists like Franz Boas and Bronisław Malinowski saw as lazy and superficial cross-cultural comparisons made by their Victorian forebears—E. B. Tylor, James Frazer, and their ilk—who themselves rarely ventured beyond their libraries, relying instead on dubious secondhand accounts of foreign cultures. Their policy was therefore to avoid comparison and generalization altogether. In later generations, the desire to construct and test general theories—including about religion—returned to anthropology, but the lesson had been imbibed that this was a daunting task, not to be undertaken lightly, if at all.

For most of the 20th and 21st centuries, psychologists have also been particularists of a sort, but only in practice, not in theory. Unlike the Victorian anthropologists, we did leave our libraries, but remained in our backyards. Even today, most of our experimental participants come from so-called *convenience samples*, which mostly comprise undergraduate students participating in exchange for course credit. This is true of some of the studies in this book, including my own work. But, quite unlike modern anthropologists, we do not refrain from jumping to conclusions about human nature more broadly. We imagine that we are learning about the psychology of religion, when what we are mostly studying is the psychology of American Protestants, who make up the lion's share of our research samples.

When cross-cultural psychological research is done, it is often done poorly. There are increasing numbers of large-scale studies that cover dozens of countries, but there is rarely any theoretical rationale for why those countries and not others were included. Furthermore, questions are often translated into different languages without conscientious checking for cultural appropriateness or any other discussion with locals. Recall the case of Pew Research Center's unwittingly Protestant translation of "God" into Chinese in Chapter 6, for example, as well as other issues mentioned there about cultural biases in measurement. We are, in other words, at risk of returning to the superficiality of our Victorian forebears. I certainly plead guilty on this charge, having contributed to this kind of scattershot the-more-the-merrier approach to cross-cultural data collection.[10] This method has its place, but it is a blunt tool.

The kind of experimental anthropology exemplified by Ben Purzycki's work can be seen as an effort to do cross-cultural psychology well, with more depth and precision, incorporating the insights of the anthropological particularists without sharing their pessimism about generalizing beyond their field sites. This approach involves establishing roots in field sites for long-term research, as well as collaborative comparative research across field sites. It involves one-off quantitative experiments informed by detailed observations of and conversations with people from local communities. This attention to cultural detail not only avoids distortions and losses in translation but also helps us to make cross-cultural comparisons that are theoretically sensible. Despite the serendipity involved in Ben's choice of field site, Tuva presented an ideal context for testing theories about the moral function of religion as Tuvan gods are not considered to be morally concerned. This provides a clear contrast against the moralizing God of American Christianity found on the University of Connecticut campus where Ben ran his other studies.

The good news is that Ben's style of experimental anthropology is growing. Since his work in Tuva, Ben has also led larger-scale projects with like-minded researchers, collecting data from field sites across multiple continents.[11] His alma mater, the University of Connecticut, now has an Experimental Anthropology Lab led by a pioneer of this approach, Dimitris Xygalatas, whose main field site is in Mauritius. Cristine Legare's team no longer does much work in Brazil but has repeatedly returned to Vanuatu. Even my own research has moved in the direction of preferring to work with an expert living in field sites, including Japan and Myanmar.[12]

Faith and hope in science

My first crisis of faith in science predates the replication crisis: it struck me early on in graduate school, while I was under the tutelage of Alan Musgrave, himself a student and colleague of Karl Popper's and Imre Lakatos's, giants of 20th-century philosophy of science. From Alan I learned about three ideas that shook me. The first is called the *underdetermination of theory of data*, and is basically the idea that empirical observations can never definitively prove theories. The second is called the *pessimistic induction*, which begins with the observation that the history of science is a graveyard of failed and abandoned theories, and leads to the conclusion that we should therefore not expect any present or future theories to survive the test of time. The third is called the *problem of verisimilitude*, which asks what it even means to say that one theory is "more true" or "closer to the truth" than another. It turns out to be very difficult to articulate a logically coherent account of this, which means that when we say, for example, that Copernicus's heliocentric theory of the cosmos is closer to the truth than Ptolemy's geocentric theory, we literally don't know what we are talking about.

There are, you might not be surprised to hear, large research literatures on all three ideas, as philosophers continue their parrying and riposting. But the impact that these ideas had on me was devastating, at least at first. Science was supposed to be a source of certain knowledge, backed up by indubitable facts: and I, a budding scientist, was supposed to be in the business of establishing those facts in the service of discovering deep truths about the world. As the seminar series progressed, however, I learned to accept the uncertainty and provisionality of science. Alan persuaded me that science can still progress toward truth, even without our ever being aware of how far or close we are, or when we have arrived.

It is difficult to say exactly how he did this, and I certainly have no knockdown argument for my belief in and commitment to science, any more than I do for my religious beliefs and commitments. It is tempting to parrot the slogan that I believe in science because it works, but this response fails to do justice to the kind of science that I care most about, which is the kind of science that tries to get at the hidden causes and structures of things, without necessarily producing any useful technologies or therapies.

I suspect that my commitment to science—including my particular subdiscipline of science—is motivated in part by something like *moral* considerations, and has something to do with humility. I am not suggesting that scientists are humbler than anyone else, but there is a kind of humility built into how science works. The subjection of ideas to empirical testing is itself one manifestation of humility: the scientific method does not allow us to presume that we are right, but compels us to check our beliefs against reality as best we can. The concern for the replicability of findings is cut from the same cloth, and so is the replication crisis itself, which emerged from a psychology's appetite for self-criticism and self-correction. To be sure, it is not any individual psychologists' willingness to subject our beliefs to the test or our findings to replication attempts that matters here, but the entire field's collective attitude.

So it is, then, that nearly a decade after the beginning of the replication crisis, I have not lost my faith in this little patch of science, less still in the scientists that work at it. We are, I believe, more aware now of the limitations of our methods, and consequently more eager to work with others across the methodological and disciplinary boundaries that artificially divide us. I can see evidence around me—among colleagues and collaborators, and especially graduate students—that we are taking steps to ensure that our findings are reliable. Our samples are getting larger and more diverse; our hypotheses and analyses are being preregistered, so that others can hold us accountable, and we are not tempted to engage in dubious statistical practices; our studies are being replicated, and failed replications are getting published.

To be sure, these improvements have been gradual and piecemeal, and the prevailing incentive structures still reward productivity and celebrity over rigor. As things stand, much of the burden rests on scientists to be guided more by curiosity and a desire to understand the world than by careerist ambition. Frankly, the odds are stacked against us: every scientist I know feels the pressure to publish, and to promote their accomplishments to their peers, to their employers and potential employers, to funding bodies, and even to the general public via various media. The material conditions of science are not conducive for the flourishing of what we might call scientific virtues. And yet, the aforementioned signs of change are encouraging. When I talk to individual scientists—the men and women we have met in this book, and more besides—about the challenges that beset us, they tend to be quietly and cautiously optimistic that we are meandering our way toward truths after all.

The proof is, as they say, in the pudding. It is still too early to say how much experimental psychologists—even in collaboration with other social scientists—can help us to understand religion as a human phenomenon. But it is important to consider the difference that this kind of research has already made, not only from the experiments that have actually been run but also from the mindset that it encourages, which is to think in experimental and more broadly empirical terms.

For many centuries, one of the most common theories of religion in the West was that Judaism and Christianity were inspired by God, whereas other religions were inspired by demons. We owe this particular idea to Justin Martyr, a Christian apologist from the second century, but it remained influential for an embarrassingly long time, until around the 18th century. It is not just Christians who had ideas that now strike us as absurd. Sigmund Freud's theory of religion revolved around men's desires to murder their fathers and the guilt that that evinces, which leads to the deification and worship of fathers in a spectacular act of overcompensation.

Not all old ideas are bad, of course. Many of the hypotheses tested in the experiments considered in this book have ancient analogues. The work of the 18th-century historian and philosopher David Hume stands out here: many of the ideas we have covered can be found in some form in his 1757 *Natural*

History of Religion, including the importance of anthropomorphism, fear, and a desire to explain natural phenomena.

What is new is that concern for empirical evidence I mentioned earlier; and not just any old empirical evidence, but that of a certain kind and standard. It is fair to say that Justin Martyr had no empirical evidence whatsoever that Greek and Roman pagans were misled by the Devil: that was sheer speculation, not to mention bald-faced prejudice. The evidential basis for Freud's theory is not much sounder: he cobbled together his clinical interviews of a handful of neurotic patients, descriptions of Australian aboriginal totemism, and Darwin's ideas about what early human societies might have been like, and put two and two together to get something quite remarkable. Even Hume's arguments relied on secondhand accounts of beliefs and practices from different cultures, and there was very little direct evidence for his central claims.

Of course, to value evidence is not to deny that evidence is hard won; nor does our willingness to subject our hypotheses to empirical testing entail that we will be able to do so. As we have seen throughout this book, the practical matter of actually testing hypotheses is fraught with difficulties, but the translation of speculative thoughts into scientifically tractable questions is itself of great value, not least for bringing discipline to discourse. We now at least have a clearer way to assess theories. I say that Hume's ideas are better than Freud's and Justin Martyr's not only because they strike me as intuitively more plausible, but because there is some experimental evidence to support them, whereas not a shred of evidence has been marshalled for the other two. Indeed, it does not seem possible to test theories about demonic influences at all.

The experimental psychologist's demand for empirical evidence is therefore our most valuable and ultimately long-lasting contribution to the effort to understand religion. Religious beliefs may well remain matters of faith, but beliefs *about* religion—its causes and consequences—are now subject to scientific investigation. We are still trying to figure out how to use scientific tools—experimental design, psychometric instruments, statistical techniques—to better understand religion. Not all of our discoveries are going to stand the test of time, and it is a fool's errand to predict which ones will. Nor is progress even guaranteed. Whether there can be a rigorous and informative experimental psychology of religion is itself an empirical question. And what kind of experimentalists would we be if we didn't try to answer it?

Notes

Chapter 1

1. The classic introduction to social psychology for a general audience is: Aronson, E., & Aronson, J. (2018). *The social animal* (12th ed.). New York, NY: Worth Publishers.
2. Galileo never explicitly claims to have run the experiment, though a vague mention of it—without reference to the Tower of Pisa—appears in *Two New Sciences*. The earliest account of Galileo performing the experiment appears in a biography by his student, Vincenzo Viviani, composed about a decade after his death. Young's description of the double-slit experiment is irregular, departing from his usual reports in omitting quantitative details. I recommend John Worrall's investigation of the latter case: he is rather scathing of Young in general. Andrew Robinson's biography of Young is a much more positive assessment.

   Robinson, A. (2006). *The last man who knew everything.* New York, NY: Pi Press.

   Worrall, J. (1976). Thomas Young and the "refutation" of Newtonian optics: A case-study in the interaction of philosophy of science and history of science. In C. Howson (Ed.), *Method and appraisal in the physical sciences: The critical background to modern science, 1800–1905* (pp. 107–179). Cambridge, UK: Cambridge University Press.
3. For example:Slater, L. (2005). *Opening Skinner's box: Great psychological experiments of the twentieth century.* New York, NY: W. W. Norton & Company.
4. Galton, F. (1872). Statistical inquiries into the efficacy of prayer. *Fortnightly Review, 12,* 125–135.
5. Benson, H., Dusek, J. A., Sherwood, J. B., Lam, P., Bethea, C. F., Carpenter, W., . . . Drumel, D. (2006). Study of the Therapeutic Effects of Intercessory Prayer (STEP) in cardiac bypass patients: A multicenter randomized trial of uncertainty and certainty of receiving intercessory prayer. *American Heart Journal, 151,* 934–942.
6. The terms "between-subjects" and "within-subjects" are standard in psychology. I don't like them.
7. Soares, C. (2006). No prayer prescription. *Scientific American.* https://doi.org/10.1038/scientificamerican0606-20a.
8. Sullivan, A., Voas, D., & Brown, M. (2014). *The art of asking questions about religion.* (CLS Working Paper 2014/4). London, UK: Centre for Longitudinal Studies.
9. Segall, M. H., Campbell, D. T., & Herskovits, M. J. (1963). Cultural differences in the perception of geometric illusions. *Science, 139,* 769–771.
10. Luhrmann, T. M., Padmavati, R., Tharoor, H., & Osei, A. (2015). Differences in voice-hearing experiences of people with psychosis in the USA, India and Ghana: Interview-based study. *British Journal of Psychiatry, 206,* 41–44.

11. Halladay, A. K., Bishop, S., Constantino, J. N., Daniels, A. M., Koenig, K., Palmer, K., . . . Taylor, J. L. (2015). Sex and gender differences in autism spectrum disorder: Summarizing evidence gaps and identifying emerging areas of priority. *Molecular Autism*, *6*, 36. https://doi.org/10.1186/s13229-015-0019-y

12. The thing about Newark is actually quite interesting. It's a quiz based on vocabulary, available here: https://www.nytimes.com/interactive/2014/upshot/dialect-quiz-map.html.

13. Burnett, D. (2013, November 29). Online IQ tests: Are they valid? *The Guardian*. Retrieved from https://www.theguardian.com/science/2013/nov/29/iq-tests-online-are-they-valid.

14. For other information on general intelligence, see: Deary, I. J. (2021). *Intelligence: A very short introduction*. Oxford, UK: Oxford University Press.

    Flynn, J. R. (2007). *What is intelligence?* Cambridge, UK: Cambridge University Press.

15. The "NEO" no longer stands for anything. It was originally an acronym for neuroticism-extraversion-openness, when the original authors, Paul Costa and Robert McCrae, were only trying to measure these three traits.

16. Ozer, D. J., & Benet-Martinez, V. (2006). Personality and the prediction of consequential outcomes. *Annual Review of Psychology*, *57*, 401–421.

17. There is an ongoing effort to compile measures of religiosity in one place: the most recent compilation of this kind was published in 1999.

    Hill, P. C., & Hood, R. W. (Eds.). (1999). *Measures of religiosity*. Birmingham, AL: Religious Education Press.

18. Nord, C. L., Gray, A., Charpentier, C. J., Robinson, O. J., & Roiser, J. P. (2017). Unreliability of putative fMRI biomarkers during emotional face processing. *NeuroImage*, *156*, 119–127.

    Lindquist, K. A., Wager, T. D., Kober, H., Bliss-Moreau, E., & Barrett, L. F. (2012). The brain basis of emotion: A meta-analytic review. *Behavioral and Brain Sciences*, *35*, 121–143.

19. Saarimäki, H., Ejtehadian, L. F., Glerean, E., Jääskeläinen, I. P., Vuilleumier, P., Sams, M., & Nummenmaa, L. (2018). Distributed affective space represents multiple emotion categories across the human brain. *Social Cognitive and Affective Neuroscience*, *13*, 471–482.

    Kragel, P. A., & LaBar, K. S. (2016). Decoding the nature of emotion in the brain. *Trends in Cognitive Sciences*, *20*, 444–455.

20. Greenwood, V. (2017). Is your happy the same as my happy? *Scientific American Mind*, *28*(2), 9. https://doi.org/10.1038/scientificamericanmind0317-9a.

21. This division of psychological processes into two categories is almost certainly an oversimplification. For a critical view, see:Keren, G., & Schul, Y. (2009). Two is not always better than one: A critical evaluation of two-system theories. *Perspectives on Psychological Science*, *4*, 533–550.

    Melnikoff, D. E., & Bargh, J. A. (2018). The mythical number two. *Trends in Cognitive Sciences*, *22*, 280–293.

22. Pahnke, W. (1963). *Drugs and mysticism: An analysis of the relationship between psychedelic drugs and the mystical consciousness* (Unpublished doctoral dissertation). Harvard University, Cambridge, Massachusetts, USA.

23. There have since been follow-up studies to the Good Friday Experiment. Doblin (1991) tracked down some of Pahnke's participants, and discovered some long-term effects of that psychedelic experience. More recently, Griffiths et al. (2006) improved on Pahnke's methodology, and found very similar results.

    Doblin, R. (1991). Pahnke's "Good Friday experiment": A long-term follow-up and methodological critique. *Journal of Transpersonal Psychology, 23,* 1–28.

    Griffiths, R. R., Richards, W. A., McCann, U., & Jesse, R. (2006). Psilocybin can occasion mystical-type experiences having substantial and sustained personal meaning and spiritual significance. *Psychopharmacology, 187,* 268–283.

24. This will not be true if you are a practitioner of Peyotism or a member of the Uranira in the Peruvian Amazon accustomed to consuming ayahuasca.

Chapter 2

1. Adam, M. (1904, July 7). Le penseur. *Gil Blas,* 1. Retrieved from https://gallica.bnf.fr/ark:/12148/bpt6k75309899.item.

2. See also Elsen, A. E. (1985). *Rodin's thinker and the dilemmas of modern public sculpture.* New Haven, CT: Yale University Press.

3. Pew Research Center. (2015). *The future of world religions: Population growth projections, 2010–2050.* Washington, DC: Pew Research Center. Retrieved fromhttps://www.pewforum.org/2015/04/02/religious-projections-2010-2050/.

4. Pew Research Center. (2016). *Religion and education around the world.* Washington, DC: Pew Research Center. Retrieved fromhttps://www.pewforum.org/2016/12/13/religion-and-education-around-the-world/.

5. Norris, P., & Inglehart, R. (2011). *Sacred and secular: Religion and politics worldwide.* Cambridge, UK: Cambridge University Press.

6. Ecklund, E. H., Johnson, D. R., Scheitle, C. P., Matthews, K. R., & Lewis, S. W. (2016). Religion among scientists in international context: A new study of scientists in eight regions. *Socius, 2,* 2378023116664353.

7. Forrest, L. F., Hodgson, S., Parker, L., & Pearce, M. S. (2011). The influence of childhood IQ and education on social mobility in the Newcastle Thousand Families birth cohort. *BMC Public Health, 11,* 895. https://doi.org/10.1186/1471-2458-11-895

8. Zuckerman, M., Silberman, J., & Hall, J. A. (2013). The relation between intelligence and religiosity: A meta-analysis and some proposed explanations. *Personality and Social Psychology Review, 17,* 325–354.

9. Strenze, T. (2007). Intelligence and socioeconomic success: A meta-analytic review of longitudinal research. *Intelligence, 35,* 401–426.

10. Hemphill, J. F. (2003). Interpreting the magnitudes of correlation coefficients. *American Psychologist, 58,* 78–79.

11. Meyer, G. J., Finn, S. E., Eyde, L. D., Kay, G. G., Moreland, K. L., Dies, R. R., . . . Reed, G. M. (2001). Psychological testing and psychological assessment: A review of evidence and issues. *American Psychologist, 56*, 128–165.

12. Zuckerman et al. (2013), p. 341.

13. Daniel Kahneman's book, mentioned in the previous chapter, provides an accessible introduction to this distinction between analytic and intuitive thinking.

    Kahneman, D. (2011). *Thinking, fast and slow.* New York, NY: Farrar, Straus, & Giroux.

14. Frederick, S. (2005). Cognitive reflection and decision making. *Journal of Economic Perspectives, 19*, 25–42.

15. Pacini, R., & Epstein, S. (1999). The relation of rational and experiential information processing styles to personality, basic beliefs, and the ratio-bias phenomenon. *Journal of Personality and Social Psychology, 76*, 972–987

16. The correlation coefficient was $r = 0.44$. Welsh, M., Burns, N., & Delfabbro, P. (2013). The cognitive reflection test: How much more than numerical ability. *Proceedings of the Annual Meeting of the Cognitive Science Society, 35*, 1587–1592.

17. Alternatives to the original CRT that require even less mathematical ability have since been developed. For example:Thomson, K. S., & Oppenheimer, D. M. (2016). Investigating an alternate form of the cognitive reflection test. *Judgment and Decision Making, 11*, 99–113.

    Sirota, M., Dewberry, C., Juanchich, M., Valuš, L., & Marshall, A. C. (2020). Measuring cognitive reflection without maths: Development and validation of the verbal cognitive reflection test. *Journal of Behavioral Decision Making.* https://doi.org/10.1002/bdm.2213

18. Szaszi, B., Szollosi, A., Palfi, B., & Aczel, B. (2017). The cognitive reflection test revisited: Exploring the ways individuals solve the test. *Thinking & Reasoning, 23*, 207–234. Bago, B., & De Neys, W. (2019). The smart System 1: Evidence for the intuitive nature of correct responding on the bat-and-ball problem. *Thinking & Reasoning, 25*, 257–299.

19. In theory, general intelligence or cognitive ability and analytic cognitive style are distinct, but CRT scores tend to be positively correlated with measure of general cognitive ability like IQ tests, with r around 0.3. There are also statistical techniques that allow us to control for the correlation between IQ and CRT when looking at their correlations with religiosity. When these are applied, researchers still find that CRT is independently correlated with religiosity. Shenhav, A., Rand, D. G., & Greene, J. D. (2012). Divine intuition: Cognitive style influences belief in God. *Journal of Experimental Psychology: General, 141*, 423–428.

    Pennycook, G., Cheyne, J. A., Seli, P., Koehler, D. J., & Fugelsang, J. A. (2012). Analytic cognitive style predicts religious and paranormal belief. *Cognition, 123*, 335–346.

20. Pennycook, G., Ross, R. M., Koehler, D. J., & Fugelsang, J. A. (2016). Atheists and agnostics are more reflective than religious believers: Four empirical studies and a meta-analysis. *PLOS One, 11*, e0153039.

21. Ritchie, S. J., & Tucker-Drob, E. M. (2018). How much does education improve intelligence? A meta-analysis. *Psychological Science, 29*, 1358–1369.

22. Dostoevsky, A. (1975). *Dostoevsky/reminiscences.* Translated from Russian by B. Stillman. New York, NY: Riverlight. (Original published in 1971.)

23. Dostoevsky, F. (2008). *The Idiot.* Translated from Russian by A. Myers. Oxford, UK: Oxford University Press. (Original published in 1869.)

24. The name "Greebles" was coined by Robert Abelson to refer to some stimuli the cognitive neuroscientist Isabel Gauthier constructed for her doctoral research at Yale University. Ploks and Glips, featured in the argument below, actually happen to be Greebles in the original experiment: they refer to the two Greeble sexes.

25. Evans, J. S. B., Barston, J. L., & Pollard, P. (1983). On the conflict between logic and belief in syllogistic reasoning. *Memory & Cognition, 11*, 295–306.

26. Toplak, M. E., West, R. F., & Stanovich, K. E. (2014). Assessing miserly information processing: An expansion of the Cognitive Reflection Test. *Thinking & Reasoning, 20*, 147–168.

    Trippas, D., Pennycook, G., Verde, M. F., & Handley, S. J. (2015). Better but still biased: Analytic cognitive style and belief bias. *Thinking & Reasoning, 21*, 431–445.

27. As mentioned above, some participants were removed from the final analysis because they expressed suspicions about what the study was about. All five of these participants were in the condition with *The Thinker*, which resulted in uneven numbers across the two conditions.

28. MacKenzie, D. (2012, April 26). Analytical thinking erodes belief in God. *New Scientist.* https://www.newscientist.com/article/dn21749-analytical-thinking-erodes-belief-in-god/.

    Grewal, D. (2012, July 1). How critical thinkers lose their faith in God. *Scientific American.* https://www.scientificamerican.com/article/how-critical-thinkers-lose-their-fa/.

    Krakovsky, M. (2012, April 26). Losing your religion: Analytic thinking can undermine belief. *Scientific American.* https://www.scientificamerican.com/article/losing-your-religion-analytic-thinking-can-undermine-belief/.

    Mooney, C. (2013, December 20). Why Obamacare could produce more atheists. *Mother Jones.* https://www.motherjones.com/politics/2013/12/why-do-atheists-exist/.

29. Joseph Simmons, Leif Nelson, and Uri Simonsohn's article was one of the first to discuss questionable research practices in psychology.

    Simmons, J. P., Nelson, L. D., & Simonsohn, U. (2011). False-positive psychology: Undisclosed flexibility in data collection and analysis allows presenting anything as significant. *Psychological Science, 22*, 1359–1366.

30. Spellman, B. A. (2012). Introduction to the special section on research practices. *Perspectives on Psychological Science, 7*, 655–656.

31. Open Science Collaboration. (2012). An open, large-scale, collaborative effort to estimate the reproducibility of psychological science. *Perspectives on Psychological Science, 7*, 657–660.

Open Science Collaboration. (2015). Estimating the reproducibility of psychological science. *Science, 349,* aac4716.

32. Doyen, S., Klein, O., Pichon, C. L., & Cleeremans, A. (2012). Behavioral priming: It's all in the mind, but whose mind? *PLOS One, 7,* e29081.

33. Bargh, J. A., Chen, M., & Burrows, L. (1996). Automaticity of social behavior: Direct effects of trait construct and stereotype activation on action. *Journal of Personality and Social Psychology, 71,* 230–244.

34. Carney, D. R., Cuddy, A. J., & Yap, A. J. (2010). Power posing: Brief nonverbal displays affect neuroendocrine levels and risk tolerance. *Psychological Science, 21,* 1363–1368.

35. Ranehill, E., Dreber, A., Johannesson, M., Leiberg, S., Sul, S., & Weber, R. A. (2015). Assessing the robustness of power posing: No effect on hormones and risk tolerance in a large sample of men and women. *Psychological Science, 26,* 653–656.

36. Dominus, S. (2017, Oct 18). When the revolution came for Amy Cuddy. *New York Times Magazine.* Retrieved from https://www.nytimes.com/2017/10/18/magazine/when-the-revolution-came-for-amy-cuddy.html.

37. Damisch, L., Stoberock, B., & Mussweiler, T. (2010). Keep your fingers crossed! How superstition improves performance. *Psychological Science, 21,* 1014–1020.

Calin-Jageman, R. J., & Caldwell, T. L. (2014). Replication of the superstition and performance study by Damisch, Stoberock, and Mussweiler (2010). *Social Psychology, 45,* 239–245.

38. http://willgervais.com/blog/2017/3/2/post-publication-peer-review.

39. Camerer, C. F., Dreber, A., Holzmeister, F., Ho, T. H., Huber, J., Johannesson, M., . . . Altmejd, A. (2018). Evaluating the replicability of social science experiments in *Nature* and *Science* between 2010 and 2015. *Nature Human Behaviour, 2,* 637–644.

40. Deppe, K. D., Gonzalez, F. J., Neiman, J. L., Jacobs, C., Pahlke, J., Smith, K. B., & Hibbing, J. R. (2015). Reflective liberals and intuitive conservatives: A look at the Cognitive Reflection Test and ideology. *Judgment & Decision Making, 10,* 314–331.

Meyer, A., Frederick, S., Burnham, T. C., Guevara Pinto, J. D., Boyer, T. W., Ball, L. J., . . . Schuldt, J. P. (2015). Disfluent fonts don't help people solve math problems. *Journal of Experimental Psychology: General, 144,* e16–30.

41. Pennycook et al. (2016).

42. Sarıbay, S. A., Yılmaz, O., & Körpe, G. G. (2020). Does intuitive mindset influence belief in God? A registered replication of Shenhav, Rand and Greene (2012). *Judgment and Decision Making, 15,* 193–202.

43. Eklund, A., Nichols, T. E., & Knutsson, H. (2016). Cluster failure: Why fMRI inferences for spatial extent have inflated false-positive rates. *Proceedings of the National Academy of Sciences, 113*(28), 7900–7905.

Chapter 3

1. Roy, M. M., & Nicholas, J. C. (2004). Do dogs resemble their owners? *Psychological Science, 15,* 361–363.

2. Kelemen, D. (2004). Are children "intuitive theists"? Reasoning about purpose and design in nature. *Psychological Science, 15*, 295–301.

3. Lamb, T. D. (2011). Evolution of the eye. *Scientific American, 305*, 64–69.

4. Alexander, D. E. (2015). *On the wing: Insects, pterosaurs, birds, bats and the evolution of animal flight.* New York, NY: Oxford University Press.

5. This idea was first proposed by the great English evolutionary theorist William Hamilton.

   Hamilton, W. D. (1964). The genetical evolution of social behaviour. II. *Journal of Theoretical Biology, 7*, 17–52.

6. Dawkins, R. (1986). *The blind watchmaker: Why the evidence of evolution reveals a universe without design.* London, UK: Norton & Company, Inc.

7. The dissertation—like many doctoral dissertations—is available online for free. The research in it has also mostly been published in a single article.

   Kelemen, D. A. (1996). *The nature and development of the teleological stance* (Unpublished doctoral dissertation). University of Arizona, Tucson, Arizona. Retrieved from https://repository.arizona.edu/handle/10150/187490.

   Kelemen, D. (1999). The scope of teleological thinking in preschool children. *Cognition, 70*, 241–272.

8. Kelemen, D. (2003). British and American children's preferences for teleo-functional explanations of the natural world. *Cognition, 88*, 201–221.

9. Schachner, A., Zhu, L., Li, J., & Kelemen, D. (2017). Is the bias for function-based explanations culturally universal? Children from China endorse teleological explanations of natural phenomena. *Journal of Experimental Child Psychology, 157*, 29–48.

10. Kelemen, D., & Rosset, E. (2009). The human function compunction: Teleological explanation in adults. *Cognition, 111*, 138–143.

11. Kelemen, D., Rottman, J., & Seston, R. (2013). Professional physical scientists display tenacious teleological tendencies: Purpose-based reasoning as a cognitive default. *Journal of Experimental Psychology: General, 142*, 1074–1083.

12. Rottman, J., Zhu, L., Wang, W., Seston Schillaci, R., Clark, K. J., & Kelemen, D. (2017). Cultural influences on the teleological stance: Evidence from China. *Religion, Brain & Behavior, 7*, 17–26.

Chapter 4

1. The oneness or unity of God is of particular importance in Judaism and Islam. The *Shema Yisrael*, perhaps the most important prayer in Judaism, begins "Hear, O Israel: the Lord is our God, the Lord is one" (Deuteronomy 6.4). Similarly, the Muslim concept of tawḥīd takes first place in the Shahada recited at each of the five daily prayers: "There is no god but God." In both cases, God's oneness is not only a rejection of polytheism, but also a claim about perfect unity within God. Christians are also monotheists, which they believe to be consistent with their Trinitarianism, insisting

that they "worship one God in trinity and the trinity in unity" (Athanasian Creed) and that the Trinity is "undivided."

2. This is not to suggest that there is perfect unity within and between the Abrahamic traditions regarding divine simplicity and what it entails. The doctrine is especially contentious within Christianity. The medieval theologian John Duns Scotus is perhaps the first important Christian thinker to reject the idea that God's attributes are identical with one another, though he retains the idea that God lacks spatial and temporal parts. More recently, Christian analytic philosophers like Alvin Plantinga and William Hasker have gone further to attack the doctrine.

3. The term is owed to an article by Justin Barrett and a subsequent book by D. Jason Slone.

    Barrett, J. L. (1999). Theological correctness: Cognitive constraint and the study of religion. *Method & Theory in the Study of Religion, 11*, 325–339.

    Slone, D. J. (2004). *Theological incorrectness: Why religious people believe what they shouldn't.* New York, NY: Oxford University Press.

4. Deuteronomy 9.10.

5. Matthew 6.9.

6. Boyer, P. (2001). *Religion explained: The evolutionary origins of religious thought.* New York, NY: Basic Books.

7. Slone (2004).

8. In *Institutes of the Christian Religion,* 1.11.8.

9. Bartlett, F. C. (1932). *Remembering: A study in experimental and social psychology.* Cambridge, UK: Cambridge University Press.

10. Bransford, J. D., & Johnson, M. K. (1972). Contextual prerequisites for understanding: Some investigations of comprehension and recall. *Journal of Verbal Learning and Verbal Behavior, 11*, 717–726.

11. Johnson, M. K., Bransford, J. D., & Solomon, S. K. (1973). Memory for tacit implications of sentences. *Journal of Experimental Psychology, 98*, 203–205.

12. Barrett, J. L., & Keil, F. C. (1996). Conceptualizing a nonnatural entity: Anthropomorphism in God concepts. *Cognitive Psychology, 31*, 219–247.

13. These examples are all taken from Barrett & Keil (1996).

14. See, for example, the work on "minimally counterintuitive concepts."

    Purzycki, B. G., & Willard, A. K. (2016). MCI theory: A critical discussion. *Religion, Brain & Behavior, 6*, 207–248.

15. Nyhof, M., & Barrett, J. (2001). Spreading non-natural concepts: The role of intuitive conceptual structures in memory and transmission of cultural materials. *Journal of Cognition and Culture, 1*, 69–100.

16. Barrett, J., & Lawson, E. T. (2001). Ritual intuitions: Cognitive contributions to judgments of ritual efficacy. *Journal of Cognition and Culture, 1*, 183–201.

    Barrett, J. (2002). Smart gods, dumb gods, and the role of social cognition in structuring ritual intuitions. *Journal of Cognition and Culture, 2*, 183–193.

17. Barrett, J. (2001). How ordinary cognition informs petitionary prayer. *Journal of Cognition and Culture, 1*, 259–269.

18. Barrett, J. L. (1998). Cognitive constraints on Hindu concepts of the divine. *Journal for the Scientific Study of Religion, 37*, 608–619.

Chapter 5

1. Nozick, R. (1974). *Anarchy, state, and utopia*. New York, NY: Basic Books.
2. Foot, P. (1967). The problem of abortion and the doctrine of double effect. *Oxford Review, 5*, 5–15.

    Thomson, J. J. (1984). The trolley problem. *Yale Law Journal, 94*, 1395–1415.
3. Thought experiments might be more common in the history of science than most people suppose. In the first chapter, I mentioned in passing that Galileo and Young may never have run their famous experiments: if so, then these were thought experiments too.
4. Schrödinger, E., & Trimmer, J. D. (1980). The present situation in quantum mechanics: A translation of Schrödinger's "cat paradox" paper. *Proceedings of the American Philosophical Society, 124*, 323–338.
5. Wimmer, H., & Perner, J. (1983). Beliefs about beliefs: Representation and constraining function of wrong beliefs in young children's understanding of deception. *Cognition, 13*, 103–128.

    Baron-Cohen, S., Leslie, A. M., & Frith, U. (1985). Does the autistic child have a "theory of mind"? *Cognition, 21*, 37–46.
6. Nonverbal versions of the false-belief task seem easier for children.

    Rubio-Fernández, P., & Geurts, B. (2013). How to pass the false-belief task before your fourth birthday. *Psychological Science, 24*, 27–33.
7. Baron-Cohen et al. (1985).
8. Wimmer and Perner also credit Jonathan Bennett's and Gilbert Harman's commentaries to the same article, but Dennett's is the clearest expression. Both Bennett and Harman are also philosophers, so my point stands.
9. Hall, D. G. (1998). Continuity and the persistence of objects: When the whole is greater than the sum of the parts. *Cognitive Psychology, 37*, 28–59.

    Rose, D., Machery, E., Stich, S., Alai, M., Angelucci, A., Berniūnas, R., . . . Cohnitz, D. (forthcoming). "The ship of Theseus puzzle." In T. Lombrozo, J. Knobe, & S. Nichols (Eds.), *Oxford Studies in Experimental Philosophy* (Vol. 3). Oxford, UK: Oxford University Press.

    Hindriks, F., & Douven, I. (2018). Nozick's experience machine: An empirical study. *Philosophical Psychology, 31*, 278–298.
10. This was in an interview with Nigel Warburton.https://www.socialsciencespace.com/2014/06/bruce-hood-on-the-supernatural/.
11. I owe the McCain example to Bruce's book *Supersense*.

    Hood, B. M. (2009). *Supersense*. London, UK: Constable & Robinson.

    For more information, see:

Milbank, D. (2000, February 19). A candidate's lucky charms. *Washington Post*. Retrieved from https://www.washingtonpost.com/wp-srv/WPcap/2000-02/19/067r-021900-idx.html.

12. The idea for the serial killer's cardigan gimmick came from Paul Rozin's research on the *moral contagion effect*, often dubbed the "Hitler's sweater" effect after an example Carol Nemerrof and Paul Rozin used in their classic paper.

   Nemeroff, C., & Rozin, P. (1994). The contagion concept in adult thinking in the United States: Transmission of germs and of interpersonal influence. *Ethos, 22*, 158–186.

13. Hood, B. M., & Bloom, P. (2008). Children prefer certain individuals over perfect duplicates. *Cognition, 106*, 455–462.

14. Keeping large marine animals in captivity is a bad idea, especially if this mostly serves to entertain tourists.

15. Hood, B., Gjersoe, N. L., & Bloom, P. (2012). Do children think that duplicating the body also duplicates the mind? *Cognition, 125*, 466–474.

16. They say "him," but Nathalia told me that the hamsters were sisters.

17. Bering, J. (2019, March 22). Conversations with my dead mother: Why we see signs and omens in everyday events. *Skeptic*. Retrieved fromhttps://www.skeptic.com/reading_room/conversations-with-my-dead-mother-why-we-see-signs-omens-in-everyday-events/.

18. Bering, J. M., & Bjorklund, D. F. (2004). The natural emergence of reasoning about the afterlife as a developmental regularity. *Developmental Psychology, 40*, 217–233.

   See also:

   Bering, J. (2002). Intuitive conceptions of dead agents' minds: The natural foundations of afterlife beliefs as phenomenological boundary. *Journal of Cognition and Culture, 2*, 263–308.

19. Bering, J. M., Blasi, C. H., & Bjorklund, D. F. (2005). The development of afterlife beliefs in religiously and secularly schooled children. *British Journal of Developmental Psychology, 23*, 587–607.

   Giménez, M., & Harris, P. (2005). Children's acceptance of conflicting testimony: The case of death. *Journal of Cognition and Culture, 5*, 143–164.

   Watson-Jones, R. E., Busch, J. T., Harris, P. L., & Legare, C. H. (2017). Does the body survive death? Cultural variation in beliefs about life everlasting. *Cognitive Science, 41*, 455–476.

   The results with adults have also been replicated in China: Huang, J., Cheng, L., & Zhu, J. (2013). Intuitive conceptions of dead persons' mentality: A cross-cultural replication and more. *International Journal for the Psychology of Religion, 23*, 29–41.

20. Forstmann, M., & Burgmer, P. (2015). Adults are intuitive mind-body dualists. *Journal of Experimental Psychology: General, 144*, 222–235.

   One of the experiments in this paper actually uses a version of Derek Parfit's teletransportation thought experiment.

21. Nielsen, M., Haun, D., Kärtner, J., & Legare, C. H. (2017). The persistent sampling bias in developmental psychology: A call to action. *Journal of Experimental Child Psychology, 162*, 31–38.

Chapter 6

1. It is implied in this formula that for every proposition q that is false, God knows that q is false. For example, if God knows that Paris is the capital of France, then God know that Versailles is not the capital of France, which is to say that God knows that "Versailles is the capital of France" expresses a falsehood.

2. These examples are taken from Lewis Carroll's nonsense poem *Jabberwocky*, Noam Chomsky's *Syntactic Structures*, and Stephen Fry and Hugh Laurie's *A Bit of Fry and Laurie*, Series 1, Episode 2.

3. Cohen, A. B., Shariff, A. F., & Hill, P. C. (2008). The accessibility of religious beliefs. *Journal of Research in Personality, 42*, 1408–1417.

4. This effect is exploited in one of the most commonly used reaction time tasks in clinical contexts, the Emotional Stroop task.

5. Exodus 25.21–22.

6. See, for example: Purzycki, B. G., Apicella, C., Atkinson, Q. D., Cohen, E., McNamara, R. A., Willard, A. K., . . . Henrich, J. (2016). Moralistic gods, supernatural punishment and the expansion of human sociality. Nature, 530(7590), 327–330.

   Lang, M., Purzycki, B. G., Apicella, C. L., Atkinson, Q. D., Bolyanatz, A., Cohen, E., . . . McNamara, R. A. (2019). Moralizing gods, impartiality and religious parochialism across 15 societies. *Proceedings of the Royal Society B, 286.* https://doi.org/10.1098/rspb.2019.0202.

7. Purzycki, B. G. (2011). Tyvan cher eezi and the socioecological constraints of supernatural agents' minds. *Religion, Brain & Behavior, 1*, 31–45.

8. Purzycki, B. G. (2013). The minds of gods: A comparative study of supernatural agency. *Cognition, 129*, 163–179.

9. Pew Research Center. (2014, March 13). *Worldwide, many see belief in God as essential to morality.* Retrieved from https://www.pewresearch.org/global/2014/03/13/worldwide-many-see-belief-in-god-as-essential-to-morality/.

   Johnson, I. (2015, March 24). Chinese atheists? What the Pew survey gets wrong. *New York Review of Books.* Retrieved from https://www.nybooks.com/daily/2014/03/24/chinese-atheists-pew-gets-wrong/.

10. These names were taken from Roland Fryer's and Steven Levitt's work on distinctively White and Black names in California. Field experiments have also found that employers are more likely to contact job applicants with typically White names than otherwise comparable applications with typically Black names. There is a section on this in Levitt's book with Stephen Dubner, *Freakonomics.*

    Fryer, R. G., Jr., & Levitt, S. D. (2004). The causes and consequences of distinctively black names. *Quarterly Journal of Economics, 119*, 767–805.

    Levitt, S. D., & Dubner, S. J. (2005). Freakonomics: A rogue economist explores the hidden side of everything. New York, NY: William Morrow.

11. Henrich, J., Heine, S. J., & Norenzayan, A. (2010). The weirdest people in the world?. *Behavioral and Brain Sciences, 33*, 61–83.

12. Rosenthal, M. F., Gertler, M., Hamilton, A. D., Prasad, S., & Andrade, M. C. (2017). Taxonomic bias in animal behaviour publications. *Animal Behaviour, 127*, 83–89.

Chapter 7

1. For the uninitiated, the eucharist is also called the Mass, the Lord's Supper, and Holy Communion. The different names can serve as a denominational shibboleth.
2. The number of those who attend Mass weekly or more is considerably higher, above 60%.

   Smith, G. A. (2019, August 5). Just one-third of U.S. Catholics agree with their church that Eucharist is body and blood of Christ. *Pew Research Center*. https://www. pewresearch.org/fact-tank/2019/08/05/transubstantiation-eucharist-u-s-catholics/.
3. The Latin Vulgate of Mark 14.22, Luke 22.19, 1 Corinthians 11.24 omit *enim*, which is redundant in any case. Latin grammarians say that *enim* was frequently used by Romans for emphasis—like "indeed" in British English—and may have been introduced into eucharistic prayer this way.
4. Very briefly: his argument against the validity of his marriage to Catherine was based on the fact that she had previously been married to his brother. Leviticus 20.21 calls such a union *unclean*, and states that it would be childless. Henry and Catherine were indeed unable to conceive an heir.
5. This was declared most clearly in Pope Leo XIII's 1896 encyclical *Apostolicae curae*, and affirmed in Josef Ratzinger's 1998 doctrinal commentary to Pope John Paul II's *Ad tuendam fidem*.
6. There is an interesting exception to this rule among Syriac Christians. The Roman Catholic Church recognizes the validity of the Liturgy of Addai and Mari despite its omission of the words of institution.
7. United States Conference of Catholic Bishops (2012, October). Celiac disease, alcohol intolerance, and the church's pastoral response. *Committee on Divine Worship Newsletter*. Retrieved from http://www.usccb.org/prayer-and-worship/the-mass/order-of-mass/liturgy-of-the-eucharist/celiac-disease-and-alcohol-intolerance.cfm.
8. Taken from https://www.astrocentro.com.br/blog/simpatias/simpatia-para-conquistar-o-boy/.
9. Taken from https://www.simpatiasonline.net/cabelo-crescer-rapido/.
10. Taken from https://www.wemystic.com.br/artigos/conheca-simpatia-para-sorte-prosperidade-e-dinheiro-rapido/.
11. Legare, C. H., & Gelman, S. A. (2008). Bewitchment, biology, or both: The co-existence of natural and supernatural explanatory frameworks across development. *Cognitive Science*, *32*, 607–642.
12. Luhrmann, T. M. (2012). When God talks back: Understanding The American evangelical relationship with God. New York, NY: Alfred A. Knopf.

Chapter 8

1. The UK ONS has a life expectancy calculator, available at https://www.ons.gov.uk/peoplepopulationandcommunity/healthandsocialcare/healthandlifeexpectancies/articles/lifeexpectancycalculator/2019-06-07.

2. See, for example:

Epley, N., Akalis, S., Waytz, A., & Cacioppo, J. T. (2008). Creating social connection through inferential reproduction: Loneliness and perceived agency in gadgets, gods, and greyhounds. *Psychological Science, 19*, 114–120.

Kay, A. C., Gaucher, D., Napier, J. L., Callan, M. J., & Laurin, K. (2008). God and the government: Testing a compensatory control mechanism for the support of external systems. *Journal of Personality and Social Psychology, 95*, 18–35.

3. The third paper is by Nathan Heflick and Jamie Goldenberg. In their experiment, they tried to persuade people to believe in an afterlife before subjecting them to a standard worldview defense experiment. They found that afterlife beliefs reduced participants' defensive nationalism. Ken Vail has since attempted and failed to replicate this finding.

Heflick, N. A., & Goldenberg, J. L. (2012). No atheists in foxholes: Arguments for (but not against) afterlife belief buffers mortality salience effects for atheists. *British Journal of Social Psychology, 51*, 385–392.

Vail, K. E., Soenke, M., Waggoner, B., & Mavropoulou, I. (2020). Natural, but not supernatural, literal immortality affirmation attenuates mortality salience effects on worldview defence in atheists. *Personality and Social Psychology Bulletin, 46*, 312–326.

4. That said, the stages were not intended to be linear.

5. For a survey of over 200 experiments, see: Burke, B. L., Martens, A., & Faucher, E. H. (2010). Two decades of terror management theory: A *meta*-analysis of mortality salience research. *Personality and Social Psychology Review, 14*, 155–195.

6. Rosenblatt, A., Greenberg, J., Solomon, S., Pyszczynski, T., & Lyon, D. (1989). Evidence for terror management theory: I. The effects of mortality salience on reactions to those who violate or uphold cultural values. *Journal of Personality and Social Psychology, 57*(4), 681–690.

7. Fritsche, I., Jonas, E., Fischer, P., Koranyi, N., Berger, N., & Fleischmann, B. (2007). Mortality salience and the desire for offspring. *Journal of Experimental Social Psychology, 43*, 753–762.

8. Vicary, A. M. (2011). Mortality salience and namesaking: Does thinking about death make people want to name their children after themselves? *Journal of Research in Personality, 45*, 138–141.

9. Greenberg, J., Kosloff, S., Solomon, S., Cohen, F., & Landau, M. (2010). Toward understanding the fame game: The effect of mortality salience on the appeal of fame. *Self and Identity, 9*, 1–18.

10. Mikulincer, M., & Florian, V. (2002). The effects of mortality salience on self-serving attributions: Evidence for the function of self-esteem as a terror management mechanism. *Basic and Applied Social Psychology, 24*, 261–271.

Dechesne, M., Pyszczynski, T., Arndt, J., Ransom, S., Sheldon, K. M., Van Knippenberg, A., & Janssen, J. (2003). Literal and symbolic immortality: The effect of evidence of literal immortality on self-esteem striving in response to mortality salience. *Journal of Personality and Social Psychology, 84*, 722–737.

11. For example:

Schimel, J., Simon, L., Greenberg, J., Pyszczynski, T., Solomon, S., Waxmonsky, J., & Arndt, J. (1999). Stereotypes and terror management: Evidence that mortality salience enhances stereotypic thinking and preferences. *Journal of Personality and Social Psychology, 77,* 905.

   Fritsche, I., & Jonas, E. (2005). Gender conflict and worldview defence. *British Journal of Social Psychology, 44,* 571–581.

   Nelson, L. J., Moore, D. L., Olivetti, J., & Scott, T. (1997). General and personal mortality salience and nationalistic bias. *Personality and Social Psychology Bulletin, 23,* 884–892.

   Greenberg, J., Schimel, J., Martens, A., Solomon, S., & Pyszczynski, T. (2001). Sympathy for the devil: Evidence that reminding Whites of their mortality promotes more favorable reactions to White racists. *Motivation and Emotion, 25,* 113–133.

   Webster, R. J., & Saucier, D. A. (2011). The effects of death reminders on sex differences in prejudice toward gay men and lesbians. *Journal of Homosexuality, 58,* 402–426.

12. Greenberg, J., Pyszczynski, T., Solomon, S., Rosenblatt, A., Veeder, M., Kirkland, S., & Lyon, D. (1990). Evidence for terror management theory II: The effects of mortality salience on reactions to those who threaten or bolster the cultural worldview. *Journal of Personality and Social Psychology, 58,* 308–318.

13. Dechesne et al. (2003) above.

   Jonas, E., & Fischer, P. (2006). Terror management and religion: Evidence that intrinsic religiousness mitigates worldview defense following mortality salience. *Journal of Personality and Social Psychology, 91,* 553–567.

14. "God (Jesus)" is how Vail et al. (2012) phrased it to clarify to the participants that they were referring to the Christian God.

15. Not everyone is going to be happy with my calling Missouri a southern state.

16. Pyszczynski, T., Greenberg, J., & Solomon, S. (1999). A dual-process model of defense against conscious and unconscious death-related thoughts: An extension of terror management theory. *Psychological Review, 106,* 835–884.

17. Routledge, C., Arndt, J., & Goldenberg, J. L. (2004). A time to tan: Proximal and distal effects of mortality salience on sun exposure intentions. *Personality and Social Psychology Bulletin, 30,* 1347–1358.

   Arndt, J., Schimel, J., & Goldenberg, J. L. (2003). Death can be good for your health: Fitness intentions as a proximal and distal defense against mortality salience. *Journal of Applied Social Psychology, 33,* 1726–1746.

18. There were two differences between this study and the previous one. The control condition here was about pain, and the order of the questions about the deities was changed so that the questions about Allah came last.

19. The control condition changed again: this time it was about social isolation.

20. Just in case you were wondering: only *two* individuals in my sample self-identified as agnostic.

21. Shariff, A., Cohen, A., & Norenzayan, A. (2008). The devil's advocate: Secular arguments diminish both implicit and explicit religious belief. *Journal of Cognition and Culture, 8,* 417–423.

22. The correlation between supernatural IAT scores and equivalent self-report measures is somewhere between 0.2 and 0.3, which is similar to other IATs. This too is

controversial. Some people take this positive but weak correlation to indicate that IATs and self-report measures assess different but related things. Others focus on the weakness of the correlation to criticize IATs for lack of convergent validity.

Ross, R. M., Brown-Iannuzzi, J. L., Gervais, W. M., Jong, J., Lanman, J. A., McKay, R., & Pennycook, G. (2019). Measuring supernatural belief implicitly using the affect misattribution procedure. *Religion, Brain, & Behavior.* https://doi.org/10.1080/21535 99X.2019.1619620.

23. Most terror management studies report no change in self-reported mood, but some recent research has detected increases in fear. Even these studies show very small changes, however: participants in the MS condition are about 10% more fearful than those in neutral control conditions, but still remain low.

Lambert, A. J., Eadeh, Fl. R., Peak, S. A., Scherer, L. D., Schott, J. P., & Slochower, J. M. (2014). Toward a greater understanding of the emotional dynamics of the mortality salience manipulation: Revisiting the "affect-free" claim of terror management research. *Journal of Personality and Social Psychology, 106,* 655–678.

24. Stetson, C., Fiesta, M. P., & Eagleman, D. M. (2007). Does time really slow down during a frightening event? *PLOS One, 2,* e1295.

Epilogue

1. Batson, C. D. (1977). Experimentation in psychology of religion: An impossible dream. *Journal for the Scientific Study of Religion, 16,* 413–418.

2. Klein, R. A., Cook, C. L., Ebersole, C. R., Vitiello, C. A., Nosek, B. A., Chartier, C. R., . . . Ratliff, K. A. (2020, September 18). Many Labs 4: Failure to replicate mortality salience effect with and without original author involvement. https://doi.org/10.31234/osf.io/vef2c.

Sætrevik, B., & Sjåstad, H. (2019, May 17). Failed pre-registered replication of mortality salience effects in traditional and novel measures. https://doi.org/10.31234/osf.io/dkg53.

Schindler, S., Reinhardt, N., & Reinhard, M. A. (2021). Defending one's worldview under mortality salience: Testing the validity of an established idea. *Journal of Experimental Social Psychology.* https://doi.org/10.1016/j.jesp.2020.104087

3. Epley et al. (2008).

4. Kay, A. C., Gaucher, D., Napier, J. L., Callan, M. J., & Laurin, K. (2008). God and the government: Testing a compensatory control mechanism for the support of external systems. *Journal of Personality and Social Psychology, 95,* 18–35.

5. Hoogeveen, S., Wagenmakers, E. J., Kay, A. C., & Van Elk, M. (2018). Compensatory control and religious beliefs: A registered replication report across two countries. *Comprehensive Results in Social Psychology, 3,* 240–265.

6. Schwarz, N., Bless, H., Strack, F., Klump, G., Rittenauer-Schatka, H., & Simons, A. (1991). Ease of retrieval as information: Another look at the availability heuristic. *Journal of Personality and Social Psychology, 61,* 195–202.

7. Iles-Caven, Y., Gregory, S., Northstone, K., & Golding, J. (2019). Longitudinal data on parental religious behaviour and beliefs from the Avon Longitudinal Study of Parents and Children (ALSPAC). *Wellcome Open Research, 4,* 38.

8. Indeed, we have done so, but that is a story for another day. Morris Trainor, Z., Jong, J., Bluemke, M., & Halberstadt, J. (2019). Death salience moderates the effect of trauma on religiosity. *Psychological Trauma: Theory, Research, Practice, and Policy, 11,* 639–646.

9. In summary, those directly affected by the earthquake were more likely to begin affiliation with a religion than to stop doing so.

   Sibley, C. G., & Bulbulia, J. (2012). Faith after an earthquake: A longitudinal study of religion and perceived health before and after the 2011 Christchurch New Zealand earthquake. *PLOS One, 7,* e49648.

10. Jong, J., Halberstadt, J., Bluemke, M., Kavanagh, C., Jackson, C. (2019). Death anxiety, exposure to death, mortuary preferences, and religiosity in five countries. *Nature Scientific Data,* 154. https://doi.org/10.1038/s41597-019-0163-x.

    Jong, J., Baimel, A., Ross, R., McKay, R., Bluemke, M., & Halberstadt, J. (2020). Traumatic life experiences and religiosity in eight countries. *Scientific Data, 7,* 140. https://doi.org/10.1038/s41597-020-0482-y.

    McPhetres, J., Jong, J., Zuckerman, M. (2020). Religious Americans have less positive attitudes toward science, but this does not extend to other cultures. *Social Psychological and Personality Science.* https://doi.org/10.1177/1948550620923239.

11. Purzycki, B. G., Apicella, C., Atkinson, Q. D., Cohen, E., McNamara, R. A., Willard, A. K., . . . Henrich, J. (2016). Moralistic gods, supernatural punishment and the expansion of human sociality. *Nature, 530,* 327–330.

12. E.g., Kavanaugh, C., & Jong, J. (2020). Is Japan religious? *Journal for the Study of Religion, Nature and Culture, 14,* 152–180.; Stanford, M., & Jong, J. (2019). Beyond Buddhism and animism: A psychometric test of the structure of Burmese Theravada Buddhism. *PLOS One, 14,* e0226414. https://doi.org/10.1371/journal.pone.0226414.

Index

For the benefit of digital users, indexed terms that span two pages (e.g., 52–53) may, on occasion, appear on only one of those pages.